Books by the same author

The Parent's Guide to the Modern World
A book about the social and society pressures on teens and preteens.

The Young Person's Guide to the Modern World
Advice for preteens and teens about coping with the pressures around them.

Gratitude at Home
A book for parents to help teach their children the ancient practice of Gratitude. Has accompanying Gratitude Journals.

Gratitude in Primary Schools
A book for primary school teachers on introducing Grattiude in the classroom. Has accompanying Gratitude Journals.

Gratitude in Secondary Schools and Higher Education
Guidance for secondary and higher educational professionals on introducing Gratitude to their students. Has accompanying Gratitude Journals.

101 Behavior Tips for Parents
Behaviour management tips for parents of children under 10.

101 Tips for Parents
Short snippets of parenting advice for parents of children under 10.

101 More Tips for Parents
More pieces of advice for parents of children under 10.

Boosting Positive Mental Health in Teens (with Naomi Richards)
An ebook containing practical strategies for parents in helping maintain positive wellbeing in teenagers.

The Gifted Introvert (with Mary Jane Boholst)
Guidance for introverts of all ages on finding the hidden gift of their personality.

A.W.O.L.

the missing teenage brain and the impact on mental health

(Strategies for parents and teachers of pre-teens or teenagers)

By Richard Daniel Curtis

©2018 Richard Daniel Curtis

All rights reserved

All rights reserved. No part of this publication may be reproduced, distributed, or transmitted in any form or by any means, including photocopying, recording, or other electronic or mechanical methods, without the prior written permission of the publisher, except in the case of brief quotations embodied in critical reviews and certain other noncommercial uses permitted by copyright law.

A copy of this book is held by the British Library.

First edition published 7/18

ISBN 13: 978-1-912010-16-5
Ebook ISBN: 978-1-912010-17-2

Published by: The Kid Calmer Ltd

Cover and internal images from pixabay.com

For more details on Richard's work, please go to www.richarddanielcurtis.com

A.W.O.L.

the missing teenage brain and the impact on mental health

By Richard Daniel Curtis

Contents

Introduction	1

Part One Adolescence

Adolescent Changes	11
Physical	13
Psychosexual	19
Psychosocial	23
Attachment	27
Spiritual	29
Summary	32
The Brain	35
Changes in the Brain during Puberty	39
Dopamine loops	43
The Impact of Puberty	49
The Impact of the Physical Changes in the Body	49

The impact of the changes of the brain	53
The Impact on Sleep	57
The Impact on Attitude	61
The Impact of Alcohol, Sex and Drugs	65
The impact on mental health	73

Part Two Mental Health Problems

Common Mental Health Problems	79
Anxiety	83
Obsessive-Compulsive Disorders	93
Eating Disorders	99
Depression	105
Psychosis	111
Self-harm	117
Suicide	119
Chronic Fatigue Syndrome	123
Loss and Grief	125
What to do if you are Concerned	131
Possible treatments	133

Part Three Other Factors Affecting Mental Wellbeing

Self-Security and Trust	141
Recognising Emotions	149
Coping with Emotions	155
Coping with Stress	161
Social Lives	169
Romantic Relationships	173
Technology	179
Online relationships	185

Part Four Strategies for Resilience and Good Mental Health

Healthy Sleep	191
Healthy Eating	195
Healthy Exercise	201
Goal Setting	205

Self-Motivation	209
Relaxation	215
Support Networks	221
Types of conversation	223
Parents	225
Teachers	227
Family	229
Mentors	231
Friends and romantic partners	233
Other professionals	235

Back Matter

References and Further Reading	241
Books	241
Research and Articles Referred to	242
About the Author	251

A.W.O.L. the missing teenage brain

Introduction

Welcome to this book about the changes in the brain of teens and preteens. There are huge changes that happen during these vital years. They have a massive impact on the functioning of the brain and in turn the mental health of our young people. Various studies have shown that during adolescence, as many as 20% of young people experience mental health problems. This book was written out of concern about the impact this has on our children.

The reality is that we all experience poor mental health at some point in our lives – it may be due to a relationship break down, stress, post-natal depression or another condition. However, as we will discuss in this book, the important thing is at these times we have the ability to communicate the emotional experience we are going through to our support network.

As both a parent and a teacher, I understand how worrying the statistics about our teenagers can be. A figure that high implies that even given our best efforts, we may not be able to avoid that happening to our children. As a result it becomes more important to understand what we can do if we do have concerns about their mental wellbeing.

The purpose of this book is to help you navigate the changes happening in their brain, the difficulties that puberty brings and to give you an understanding of what common teenage mental health conditions look like.

The book is split into four parts. The first focuses on adolescence. Our understanding of puberty has developed enormously over last 20 years. Technology in Magnetic Resonance Imaging (MRI – the use of magnetic fields and radio waves to produce an image of the inside of the body), Functional MRIs (the measurement of brain activity) and diffusion tensor imaging (DTI – a measurement of flow throughout the brain) has improved tremendously over the last 20 years. This has revolutionised our understanding of the changes that happen before, during and after puberty. In this part of the book we'll discuss our understanding of the significant changes happening in this vital period of life.

Introduction

Beginning with the physical changes during puberty, we will continue onto discussing the changes in the brain. We will then explore the impact of these changes on our children, what happens during this period with our sleep cycles and the impact on their attitude. Finally, we will discuss the impact of alcohol, drugs and sex on their development.

In Part Two, I will share information on some of the most commonly diagnosed mental health conditions that adolescents experience. I will mention common treatments and what to watch out for.

We will cover:

- Anxiety;
- Obsessive Compulsive Disorder;
- Eating Disorders;
- Depression;
- Psychosis;
- Self-harm;
- Suicide;
- Chronic Fatigue Syndrome;
- Loss and Grief.

Finally, we will discuss what to do if you are concerned about your child and common sources of support when you are concerned the difficulties are no longer low-level difficulties.

Part Three focuses on other factors that would affect a young person's ability to cope with low-level mental health problems. We will begin with a discussion on self-security and trust, two vital concepts for maintaining positive mental wellbeing.

Continuing with an exploration of recognising and coping with emotions, we will explore these vital aspects of mental wellbeing. We will also talk about ways that our young people can cope with the increased stress they are under.

This is then followed by chapters on external factors that affect the wellbeing of our children. First, their social relationships – a huge influence on young people's mental health. Secondly, we will discuss the impact of romantic relationships and finally the impact of technology on the emerging brain.

Part Four focuses on practical tips that you can use in everyday life to help ensure that the support networks and outlets that help to avoid the negative impact of mental health difficulties do not become overwhelming for your child.

We will cover healthy sleep, eating and exercise habits. It is important that adolescents are able to set their own goals and work towards them; we'll discuss some strategies for supporting them. A chapter of self-motivation, an important consideration in the teenage years, will follow this.

We will discuss how to help young people to switch off and relax, to enjoy down time – a vital technique in avoiding the overwhelm of emotions. This will then be followed by ways that our children can access their vital support networks, be they parents, teachers, mentors, professionals or other friends and family.

Finally, a note on wording, throughout this book I regularly refer both to puberty and to adolescence. I aim to use these phrases interchangeably; however, there will be occasions where I inform the reader of slight differences between the two (for example during my discussion on the physical changes that are happening throughout this period).

A.W.O.L. the missing teenage brain

I have written this book for you, the adults. The more that I can help you to understand what is happening in their world, the more I can empower you to support your child and alleviate the pressure they are under.

Happy reading!

Introduction

A.W.O.L. the missing teenage brain

Part One
Adolescence

A.W.O.L. the missing teenage brain

Adolescent Changes

There are many changes, both physical and cognitive, that occur during the transition from childhood to adult. Academics have come up with a number of different theories over the years have come up with different views. Each of these holds their own place in understanding the complex nature of a child's development in adolescence and whether they are developing at the right rate.

Broadly speaking these are physical, cognitive, psychosexual, psychosocial, attachment and spiritual.

A.W.O.L. the missing teenage brain

Physical

Physical development is the recognition that, within acceptable variance, children develop at their own rate. Some will mature earlier than others will for example. The developmental theorist Arnold Gesell (the first school psychologist in the United States) developed a range of measures to be able to assess the 'maturity' of a child according to what they could and could not do. There is a version of his scale in use today that gives a child's physical development an age bracket. Children go through adolescence at different rates and so it can be hard to compare children (even siblings) as like for like.

Early adolescence and puberty is linked to three separate changes in the body. The first is a growth spurt, the second is activation of the sexual organs and the third the development of secondary sexual factors.

Growth spurt

The growth spurt will often happen at around the age of 12 for girls and 14 for boys. Average annual growth goes from about 5cm a year, to 8.3cm a year for females and 9.5cm a year for males whilst they go through puberty.

For girls the stage begins with the enlargement of the breasts. It takes about two years to reach the highest rate of growth; it is generally only after this that they start menstruating. Following this they normally only grow another 5-10cm.

Boys begin with the enlargement of the testicles, the penis does not grow for another one-two years. They do not generally finish their growth spurt until they are 20.

Because of this growth spurt, it is not uncommon for young people to become clumsy. This is because the brain can struggle to keep up with the accelerated physical growth, causing them to be unbalanced.

Sexual organ activation

The activation of sexual organs is known as *gonadarche* and marks the 'formal' start of puberty if such a thing exists. This second stage of puberty begins between the ages of 8 and 14 in females and 9-15 in males. Earlier puberty in girls can be inherited from early puberty in their mother (see Susman & Dorn, 2012).

It consists of an activation of the gonads (either the ovaries or the testes), prompted by the release of hormones. In turn, this increases the production of the sex steroids, *testosterone* (the male sex hormone) and *estradiol* (the female sex hormone).

For males, testosterone stimulates the sexual drive, and can also cause acne to develop. It is also responsible for bone strengthening and changes the shape of the pelvis (making it narrower and longer). The number of red blood cells increases because of the testosterone too.

Estradiol, the female sexual hormone, is responsible for the extra storing of fats around the body (such as in the breasts, vagina or uterus). It helps the strengthen bones and causes the pelvis to widen for potential childbirth later in life.

Secondary sexual characteristics

The third event is known as *adrenarche*, which involves the development of secondary sexual characteristics, such as body odour, sweat glands or pubic hair growth – often happening just prior to the *gonadarche* stage.

For boys, pubic hair generally starts to develop around thirteen and a half. Hair on the face and arms, development of acne and deepening of the voice happens around the age of fifteen.

Girls develop pubic hair not long after the breasts develop and hair develops under their arms around 12 years old.

Adrenarche is separate from *gonadarche*, one can happen without the other. *Adrenarche* does not necessarily include the activation of the gonads, or production of testosterone and estradiol. This means that someone who goes through *adrenarche* is not necessarily able to reproduce.

Summary

It was not until as late as 1898 that an early psychologist, James Mark Baldwin, began writing about children's cognitive skills continuing to develop after young childhood. Piaget, Erikson and many others since then, more famously later picked up this work around the development of thinking skills. In adolescence, there are many changes happening to the physical brain (see below) and this has an effect on the way that children use their brain and respond. As a result of the ability to undertake MRI scans, we are able to understand a great deal more about the way learns and adapts to situations, showing that cognitive development of the physical brain continues throughout life and the cognitive development of the mind (called the "Theory of Mind") continues well into early adulthood (see Dumontheil, Apperly and Blakemore, 2009).

Therefore, when it comes to considering whether a child is developing physically well, as you can see, there are a large number of aspects to consider. Often, a child having trouble in one area, can then have an impact on the others.

A.W.O.L. the missing teenage brain

Psychosexual

Sigmund Freud, the founder of psychoanalysis, is credited with developing the theory of psychosexual development. He proposed a theory that children go through a number of stages of development linked to sexuality – the Oral, Anal and Phallic Stages – prior to the age of five, and then enter a period of Latency until puberty. After this, he felt that people enter the Genital Stage of psychosexual development, where the ego seeks gratification through friendships, love and family. More recently, (although it did exist to some extent prior to Freud) the field of Sexology studies the development of human sexuality.

Freud believed that infants under the age of one go through a stage of satisfying their libido by putting objects in their mouth. For some, this can be observed at later life through behaviours such as nail biting, smoking, chewing pens or thumb sucking.

The next stage of Freud's theory is the Anal Stage – typified by the battle of potty training, between one and three years. He believed that the restriction put on a child by their parents about where they can go to the toilet. Someone who experiences regimented or harsh potty training, he hypothesised, resulted in them growing up to become tidy, punctual and respectful of authority – anally retentive. On the other hand, someone who experienced liberal potty training, grows up to be over friendly and shares with many people – they are anal expulsive.

During the following stage of Freud's theory, the Phallic Stage, a child becomes aware of the physical differences between boys and girls. He hypothesised that between the age of three to six years, children become obsessed with genitalia and masturbation. By the end of this stage, he felt that children develop the characteristics of their same-sex parent.

You may be familiar with an important part of Freud's theory of this stage – the Oedipus Complex. This comparison to the Greek myth, where Oedipus kills his father and ends up marrying his mother, Freud felt described the battle a child has to try and possess his mother.

Karl Jung, the Swiss Psychiatrist and Psychoanalyst, coined the phrase the Electra Complex to describe Freud's view that girls at this stage have penis envy and are father-fixated.

These two theories cause great debate about whether they happen for all children, especially when considering different cultures.

From the age of six until puberty, Freud felt children become sexually dormant throughout the Latency Stage.

The final stage of Freud's theory is the Genital Stage, where the person experiments with sexual pleasure involving others. He felt this began in puberty and ended when settled in a relationship in the late teens or twenties.

A.W.O.L. the missing teenage brain

Psychosocial

The basis of psychosocial development as developed by Erikson and others is that at each stage of a person's life there are a number of social 'tasks' that need to be completed. He phrased these as crises (1959):

Age	Psychosocial crisis
0-1.5	Trust vs. mistrust
1.5-3	Autonomy vs. Shame, Doubt
3-5	Initiative vs. Guilt
5-12	Industry vs. Inferiority
12-18	Identity and Repudiation (reject or refusal) vs. Identity Diffusion
18-40	Intimacy and Solidarity vs. Isolation
40-65	Generativity vs. Self-absorption
65+	Integrity vs. Despair

Another psychologist, Marcia (1966) further explored Erikson's views about adolescence and identified four identity statuses during latter childhood and adolescence:

> **Foreclosure** – when a young person's identity is formed by their parents (or negatively identical/opposite).

> **Identity diffusion** – the period when an adolescent is not committed to decisions, identity or even exploration of identity.
>
> **Moratorium** – time(s) when a young person is going through crisis, so not committed or only vaguely as the world is so unpredictable for them.
>
> **Identity achievement** – once the crisis period is over, the young person has made a commitment to their identity.

Peter Blos (1967) wrote about this time as a period of transformation, where the adolescent has to coordinate a growing need for their own independence, with a need to maintain their relationship with their parents. Anna Freud, the youngest daughter of Sigmund Freud and a psychanalyst, wrote about the combination of biological factors and the socialisation processes happening during this age. Finally, the psychiatrist and psychoanalyst Harry Stack Sullivan believed that development happens within the context of social interactions and those interpersonal needs are important.

Looking at these theories, it is clear how well they describe the crisis, in different ways, facing teenagers – finding their own identity and the threat of losing it amongst the many others in the world around them.

A.W.O.L. the missing teenage brain

Attachment

Attachment theory describes the way that infants bond with their main parental figures in the first few years of life affects the way they feel about themselves and those around them throughout their lives. Developed by the psychiatrist John Bowlby in the 50s and 60s, this theory focussed on the concept that humans are born with a pre-disposition to attach to someone in order to help them survive.

Prior to this, it had been believed that children were conditioned to bond with their major attachment figure (normally the mother) because of being fed and being cared for (so it is learned). Whereas attachment theory postulates that the infant is pre-programmed to want to attach to the figure because they will help them survive. Bowlby hypothesised that if a child did not attach within the first five years of their life there would be lifelong implications for them. Certainly, attachment theory is now used in as a basis for understanding many interpersonal relationships throughout childhood and into adulthood.

During the adolescent years, children move from focussing on a trusting relationship with their parents, to balancing the demands of their parents with their friendships. As they move into middle and later adolescence, romantic partners add another dimension to this pressure on teens, as they seek to maintain their attachment to their parents, their friendship circles and their romantic relationships.

Spiritual

Spiritual development (or Transpersonal Psychology) is the development of faith as a concept. It is not necessarily linked to a religion and can vary in its nature according to the child's family and their culture. This is closely linked to moral development, another topic studied by psychologists.

Kohlberg (1958) developed a six-step theory based on the earlier work of Piaget (1932) on the subject:

Level 1 – Preconventional level	Stage 1	Behaviour is determined by consequences.
	Stage 2	Behaviour is determined by gaining rewards or satisfying personal needs.
Level 2 – Conventional level	Stage 3	Behaviour is determined by social approval from others.
	Stage 4	Society laws and social rules govern behaviour.
Level 3 – Principled level	Stage 5	Individuals make decisions within (and sometimes outside of) the laws/rules in order to meet their needs.

| | | Decisions are governed by |
| | Stage 6 | ethical principles of the individual. |

Fowler (1981) proposed six stages of the development of faith, all based on the foundation of having underlying primal faith – a sense of meaning and purpose:

Stage 1 Age 2	Intuitive-projective	Interacting with others, spiritual beliefs inherited from parents.
Stage 2 School age	Mythical-literal	Accept the religious stories they hear literally. Develop a sense of good/bad and fairness. Fundamentalists remain at this level throughout most of their lives.
Stage 3 Early adolescence (may happen as late as 20s or 30s)	Synthetic-conventional	A shift from self-centred belief to an all-encompassing belief in their faith. May struggle to understand the belief systems of others. Can think of Stage 4 people as a backwards step as their

		own faith is strongly held.
Stage 4 Young-adulthood	Individuative-Reflective	Develop an understanding of other belief systems. May question their own faith. May result in becoming non-religious.
Stage 5 Mid-life	Conjunctive Faith	Recognise the limits of logic and accept the paradoxes. They remain grounded in their faith, whilst accepting the mysteries of spiritual belief.
Stage 6	Universalizing Faith	A stage that few people achieve. A devotion to serving others, such as a priest or religious figure.

Summary

As can be seen, there are various differing viewpoints on the changes (and challenges) facing children as they go through the period from middle childhood through to early adulthood. They have to face social changes, the development of their own spiritual beliefs and the separation of their secure attachment to their parents to friends and romantic partners. This combined with their physical and sexual development means that a teenager's sense of identity will change multiple times during this period and will continue to do so well into their twenties.

Some parents become concerned that their child is an early or late developer. There are a number of different factors to consider when asking ourselves "is my child's development normal?" When working with young people professionals will look at the various factors and avoid thinking of their development as normal or abnormal. The reality is various aspects of everyone's lives develop at different rates, what is normal for one child is not for the next.

Key points from this chapter

- Physical changes happen in three stages:
  - A growth spurt,
  - Activation of sexual organs,
  - Development of secondary sexual characteristics.
- Psychosexual theories suggest that during adolescence, young people move towards seeking to be involved in sexual pleasure with others.
- That psychosocially adolescents are battling with finding their own identity and seeking independence from their parents.
- That young people will seek to keep their attachment to their parents, whilst also seeking bonds with friends and romantic partners.
- That spiritual development happens over time and may not necessarily include religious beliefs.

A.W.O.L. the missing teenage brain

The Brain

Adolescence brings around a number of important changes in the physical makeup of the brain. However, in order to be able to understand why those changes matter, we need to go through a bit of basic physiology.

The brain is commonly split into three regions, the Reptilian Complex (the lizard brain), the Paleomammalian Complex (the animal brain) and the Neomammalian Complex (the human brain) based on the theories of the physician and neuroscientist Paul D MacLean in the 1960s. Although the brain is more complex than this, it is a simple effective way of considering the various functions of the brain.

The Reptilian Complex generally is considered to refer to the brain stem (the hindbrain) and the *Cerebellum*. The brain stem includes the *Medulla Oblongata* (the part of the brain that deals with automated body functions) and the *Pons* (a part of the brain that takes and feeds information from both hemispheres through to the *Cerebellum*. The *Cerebellum* is the part of the brain just above the back of your neck, which controls and fine-tunes motor controls throughout your body. The concept is that the Reptilian Complex is predominantly automated, unless the other parts of the brain require it to do something.

The Paleomammalian Complex (also known as the limbic system) refers to the central area of the brain including the *Hypothalamus*, the *Amygdalae*, the *Hippocampus* and the *Thalamus*. The *Thalamus* is the part of the midbrain that receives information from around the body and directs it to the correct part of the brain. The *Hypothalamus* is the lower frontal region associated with the thalamus and primarily is linked with triggering the release of hormones linked to emotional reactions. The two *Amygdalae* play an important role in processing emotional reactions and memories related to strong emotions. The *Hippocampi* are either side of the brain and help to consolidate short-term memories into longer term ones.

The Neomammalian brain consists of the cerebrum – two hemispheres containing the *Occipital, Temporal, Parietal* and

Frontal lobes. The *Occipital* lobes are responsible for visual processing, the Parietal lobes with sensory information, navigation and spatial awareness. The *Temporal* lobes are concerned with long-term memories, object recognition and speech comprehension. The *Frontal* lobes (including the *prefrontal cortex*) is the region of the brain related to personality, beliefs, judgement, decision-making, motivation, planning and other higher-level thinking skills.

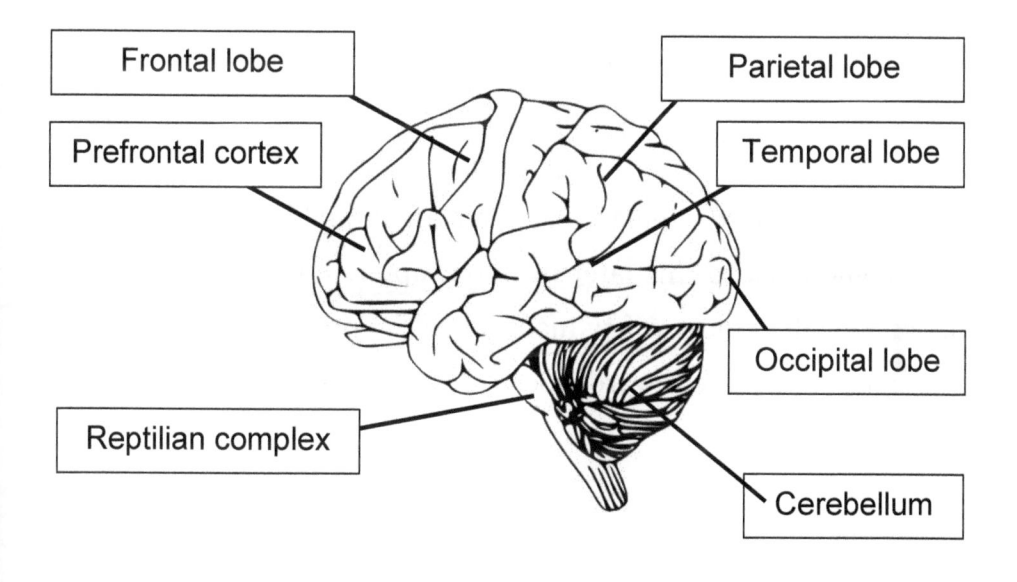

Diagram labels: Frontal lobe, Prefrontal cortex, Reptilian complex, Parietal lobe, Temporal lobe, Occipital lobe, Cerebellum.

The different functions of regions of the brain are important because there are times when faced with threat, fear or danger that people experience an automated limbic system response. You may have come across these as flight, fight or freeze responses. These are situations, where for whatever reason; the brain has interpreted the data coming in as a serious threat and triggered a response from the *amygdalae* and the *hypothalamus*. As you will see from the descriptions above, this results in the human brain being bypassed and the animal brain triggering a response, with the lizard brain deciding to tell the body to run, fight or hide. If they are going to run away from a sabre toothed tiger, then this is a very important response, the difficulty is that in the modern world there are not actually that many scenarios that warrant a reaction like that.

If someone is feeling insecure or anxious, for any reason, then their brain is more likely to react with an animal brain response, we'll come back to this later in this chapter. Further on in this book, we will explore a few mental health conditions that these reactions contribute towards too.

Changes in the Brain during Puberty

The brain goes through a number of extraordinary changes during adolescence, in much the same way as it did when they were a toddler. Prior to the onset of puberty, the brain goes through the second surge of *synaptogenesis* for a few months. This is a stage of the development of new neurons and synapses (the connectors between two brain cells) in the grey matter, particularly the frontal lobes. The grey matter are the folded bits on the outside of the brain (white matter is formed of the fibres that connect them) and in the frontal lobes, this is where the pre-frontal cortex is situated. For the child going through this stage, it is important that they be exposed to lots of new experiences, learning opportunities and unfamiliar situations to help connect these new neurons. Think of this stage as millions of new homes being built in the brain, by exposing the growing brain to new experiences, you are connecting the roads in-between the empty homes. This is important, as during the next stage, those empty unconnected homes will be demolished.

By the end of this pre-puberty phase, Blakemore and Choudhury (2006) identify that the brain has more brain cells than they will at adulthood. Once the brain hits puberty, the unused cells are ruthlessly eliminated over the next few years, this can account for up to 15% of the brain's grey matter. The frequently used cells have their connections strengthened. As Giedd and colleagues (1999) identify the frontal cortex reaches their maximum density of brain cells at the age of 12 for boys and 11 for girls. However, as the brain rewires the various parts of the brain, it leaves the prefrontal cortex until last. This effectively, shuts down the frontal lobes or inhibits their use during the pubescent years.

When you think about the roles of the prefrontal cortex described above, let us consider the main adult complaints about teenagers – moodiness, lack of communication, loss of eye contact, react to things as though it is a threat – I am sure you can now see the cause.

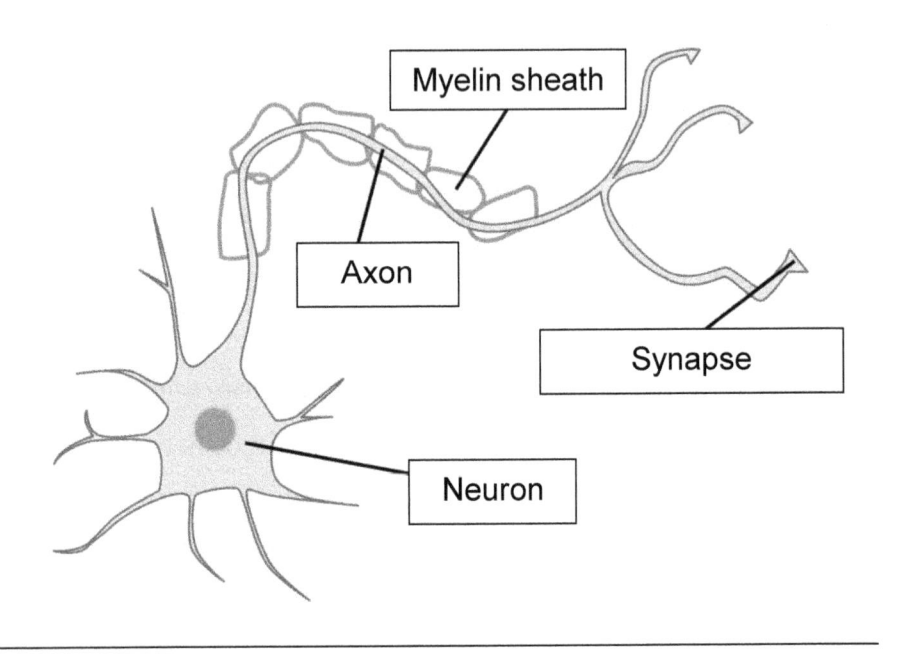

At the latter stages of puberty and through until the mid-twenties, the brain starts to strengthen the connections between the brain cells. This begins with a coating of the *axons* – these are the 'roads' that connect the brain cell with the synapses, the connectors between different cells. This coating and strengthening is called *myelination* and can speed up the transfer of messages by up to one hundred times.

A.W.O.L. the missing teenage brain

Dopamine loops

Something that most people experience is a condition known as a *dopamine loop*. *Dopamine* is a hormone that helps use with motivation, mood, attention, sleep and much more. It is effectively a seeking drug that helps you persevere to get the reward you are looking for. This is a very useful attribute for a cave dweller going out hunting and needing to stay awake all night waiting for their prey. The reward they then get from killing the prey releases *opioids* in the brain and gives them a huge rush of pleasure, reducing the dopamine level at the same time. It is the same feeling people get when they have achieved something they have been working towards for some time, maybe getting the job of their dreams, or even something as simple as winning a game.

However, the modern world has a negative impact on this natural cycle. Technology means that people expect instant feedback. People can tell when a message has been delivered to the recipient and even when they have read it. Social media often even tells users when the recipient is typing.

Now, when people send a message they seek a response, feedback or an acknowledgement. They send the message - their dopamine level rises; they see it is delivered – their dopamine level rises; they see they have read it – their dopamine level rises as they await the response. You see the pattern.

The problem is that this elevates the dopamine to a level where, even when someone does get a pleasure rush, it is not enough to counteract the raised dopamine level. Therefore, they keep checking their phone for new messages – the light is not blinking, so they swipe the screen to look for notifications, still nothing – so they open up the messages app and hit refresh, in case there is one waiting for them. Their brain is on a relentless pursuit for the satisfaction of receiving a message. Even when they do, because the dopamine level is so high, the pleasure they get isn't enough and so they reply straight away, hoping that the recipient will reply just as quickly and give them the reward they are seeking (even if they do then it's still often not enough).

The solution for dopamine loop is to have time away from what is causing the dopamine to rise. If it is work, people have weekends or holidays (this syndrome is also why it takes a few days to relax when people go for a break). If it is technology, then it is important to have time away from devices. As adults it is easier to recognise this effect (but not always), however for children this is an important part of learning about life, work and technology. They should regularly have time away from devices, to help reset their dopamine levels to normal.

Key points from this chapter

- The brain consists of three parts:
    - the reptilian complex (the lizard brain),
    - the paleomammalian complex (the animal brain),
    - and the neomammalian complex (the human brain).
- The brain can interpret some incoming information as a threat and trigger a fright, flight or freeze response.
- Millions of new cells grow in the brain prior to puberty.
- During puberty, the brain closes down functioning of parts of the human brain whilst it rewires the region.
- Throughout puberty up to 15% of the grey matter can be culled.
- The prefrontal cortex is switched back on during the latter stages of puberty.
- During the late teenage years and early twenties the connections between brain cells are strengthened.
- Dopamine loops affect hormone levels in the brain and reduce the pleasure of reward.

The Brain

A.W.O.L. the missing teenage brain

The Impact of Puberty

The Impact of the Physical Changes in the Body

The early development of puberty in boys and girls can have an impact on their development and wellbeing. Multiple studies have linked early puberty with smoking, drinking and drug use. Van Jaarsveld, Fidler, Simon and Wardle (2007) found that earlier adolescence was linked to more sedentary behaviour and higher stress levels. They also found that those going through later adolescence were less likely to skip breakfast – something that could affect their behaviour in the classroom and their academic performance.

In girls there are two maturity stages – the first period and the psychosocial maturity. The gap between the two has widened over the last two hundred years and girls experience their first period at a much younger age than they did. However, interestingly this younger age actually matches the age that it is thought girls experienced their first period 20,000 year ago. Girls who are overweight in younger childhood are more likely to start their periods earlier. Unfortunately, early onset of puberty for girls is linked to later obesity too (although not for boys).

In terms of mental health, a study by Susman & Dorn (2012) found a link between an early first period and high levels of stress. A study by Ge, Conger & Elder (2001a) found that early maturing girls report more negative or depressive emotions.

Early first periods are also related to risky social behaviour. It has been linked to earlier dating of men (who tend to be older) (Kim, Smith & Palermiti, 1997) and Ellis et al (1999) found it is related to early sex, marriage and childbirth. They also found that in turn, this leads to a higher likelihood of divorce and lower involvement rates from the father in raising their children. Early puberty has also been linked to alcohol use during adolescence, particularly if they experience lower levels of supervision.

Research surrounding changes in the age of boys' pubescent maturity are currently uncertain. Thinking about the mental health of boys, Ge, Conger & Elder (2001b) found that early maturing boys report feelings that are more hostile and a higher level of internalised distress. Another report (Kaltiala-Heino, Kosunen & Rimpela, 2003) found that early developing boys experience higher levels of depression. Although, if a boy goes through puberty quicker they are less likely to experience depression. Boys experiencing early puberty, who also experience family problems or poverty, have been found to be more likely to use alcohol.

Key points from this chapter

- There are risk factors associated with the early onset of puberty.
- Girls are generally experiencing their first period at a younger age.
- Early first periods can be associated with problems.
- Boys experiencing early puberty experience higher levels of depression.
- Boys going through puberty quickly are less likely to experience depression.

The impact of the changes of the brain

The first time a change in the wiring of the brain occurred like this was during much earlier childhood (think about those terrible temper tantrums during the toddler years). Therefore, it is reasonable to expect to see a child experience the same difficulties – tantrums, inability to get their message across, and a struggle to do things they were able to do in the past or even the complete lack of ability to explain what their problem was in the first place.

Much of this is related to the 'shutting down' of the prefrontal cortex. Just as when they were small, when a teenager experiences high levels of demands or emotions, they can feel overwhelmed and struggle with making a decision or acting. Tasks like tidying a room, resolving friendship problems and sometimes even talking about their day cause the little free space their frontal lobes to become full and the emotional brain to react.

Another very noticeable effect of the changes during adolescence is in the activities a teenager chooses to do. During these years, teenagers will often seek thrills, be it adrenaline-pumping music or rides, or more risky behaviour like sex or drugs. There is a predisposition to seek excitement and arousal. Their brain seeks sensory overload through music, games or films like horror or action.

This may be pushed to extremes within their social circle, where it is a combined with a desire to impress their friends or not show any signs of weakness. With the changes in the frontal lobes, their judgement making and risk management skills are reduced. This can lead to some very risky behaviour as the group eggs each other on or strives to be 'top dog'.

When it comes to their emotional reactions, during puberty teenagers are also likely to feel more intense and sudden emotions, Dahl (2003) describes an experiment that showed whilst all 13 year old boys were just as likely to be argumentative with their parents, those going through puberty were likely to become angrier quicker. The brain relies more on the emotional brain to react, just as though it were under threat or they felt more insecure. This highlights the huge impact the rewiring of the brain has on the teenager, as the mammalian and reptilian brain processes things that previously the levelheaded frontal lobes would have calmly dealt with. The example of this that many parents will be familiar with is the emotional reaction to a request to tidy their room – even if it is a task they have been doing for many years very successfully.

Depression is often linked to puberty and there are a number of factors relating to the physical changes happening linked to the condition. The sexual hormones released during puberty affect the release of the hormone *serotonin* (a mood regulator) in the brain. *Serotonin* is important, as it is a *neurotransmitter* – a carrier of signals between the nerves. It also regulates people's mood and arousal. Poor *serotonin* regulation is also linked to depression. A 2006 study in New Zealand found that young people with acne were more likely to suffer with depression and attempt suicide. In a link to an earlier thread, there is also evidence (Kosunen et al., 2003) of a link with depression in teenagers and multiple sexual partners plus non-use of contraception. The authors noted that this applied both ways round, that multiple sexual experiences, combined with lack of contraception could be an indicator of existing depression, but in turn could also lead to depression. We will go through more about depression later in this book, but it is easy to see how depression can play a part in so many young people's lives.

Key points from this chapter

- The shutting down of the prefrontal cortex affects young people during adolescence.
- This can affect problem-solving, social interactions, judgement making and risk taking.
- The teenage brain will seek adrenaline-fuelled activities.
- These changes will also affect emotional responses.
- Depression can be linked to puberty and there is a link to a disruption of serotonin levels.

The Impact on Sleep

The twenty-four hour cycle humans go through (including the sleep cycle) is called the *circadian rhythm*. Apart from setting when people feel tired, it also sets their sleep period. During the ages of nine to ten years, the required sleep cycle is approximately 8 hours a day, not too dissimilar to the adult sleep requirements. However, during the teenage years (and into the early twenties) this can increase to an average of nine and a half hours a day.

With the move to secondary school, many education systems keep school start times the same, or even move them earlier. However, during adolescence, the sleep cycle can also be triggered up to two hours later – think about the teenager who is wide-awake when the rest of the family are going to bed. This is due to the delayed release of a hormone called *melatonin*. Another factor that affects the release of this sleep-inducing drug is the use of screens late at night, in addition to bright room lighting (likewise, bright light in the morning shifts sleep patterns earlier). *Melatonin* is a hormone released mostly in the evening when it is approaching someone's normal bedtime and then remains at quite a high level overnight, dropping to almost nothing during the daytime.

The impact of this shift in the sleep cycle means that when young people are getting up they are part way through their *Rapid Eye Movement* period of sleep. This period of sleep, which often the teenage brain does not get, is vital for long-term memory and brain development.

Humans sleep in cycles with several periods of brief awakening and the deeper sleep states, including REM sleep, which can account for up to 25% of someone's sleep. The sleep cycle is between 90 and 120 minutes, with more cycles happening in the early hours of the morning (which equates to more REM sleep). Lack of sleep has been linked to a number of conditions, such as depression, obesity, anxiety and alcohol use.

Many teens develop coping mechanisms, for example two patterns of sleep – weekday and weekend. During the weekend, for example, adolescents will often go to bed 1-2 hours later than during the week, a habit Crowley and Carskadon (2007) refer to as "weekend bedtime delay". They also quote a US poll that found that up to 70% of adolescents rely on their parents to wake them up during the week. This additional sleep at weekends allows the adolescent to experience rebound REM sleep – more REM sleep to make up for the lost REM sleep (although not as much).

Morgan (2005) give four possible reasons for these sleep changes:

1. That millions of years ago it was beneficial for a young strong adolescent to stay awake to protect the tribe.

2. That the amount of rewiring needed means the teenager needs more sleep.

3. That teenagers are so busy in the evening that they do not allow their brains to get tired.

4. That the longer period of sleep is beneficial to the growth happening.

Many people find themselves in the routine of being either an early riser or a night owl. Night owls are more likely to suffer educationally (possibly due to the times of the school day) and are more likely to display antisocial behaviour. Girls, who like to work late at night, are more likely to experience depression and anxiety, this is worse if they are also obese.

Key points from this chapter

- Sleeping patterns are disrupted by puberty.
- Melatonin is naturally released up to two hours later during this phase.
- Melatonin release is also delayed by screens and bright lighting.
- This later sleeping pattern can disrupt REM sleep cycles.
- Teenagers often develop two patterns of sleep to cope.

The Impact on Attitude

As a young person matures, they do their best to establish their identity away from their parents. This is especially the case of other-sex parents, where it is hypothesised the subconscious pushes the young away to avoid incestuous feelings. For the parent, this stage can feel like they are not being listened to or respected, as their child does the best, it can to get around their rules and live their own life.

This is even more significant when we think about the changes happening in the brain and frontal cortex. As we discussed earlier, the brain is more likely to respond to simple things as a threat. They will struggle to hold conversation at times, their eye level will drop and the young person will use monosyllabic phrases in response to questions. Therefore, if you consider your child's attitude from a sexual or brain development perspective, you will be left with a child who appears defiant, rude and challenging.

On top of this, there is another war raging in the brain, *dopamine*. Initially, during the growth stage of brain development, there is an abundance of *dopamine* produced. During later puberty, the brain finds it harder to produce *dopamine*, and so it takes more excitement and stimulation for the teenager to experience pleasure. This explains why they like *adrenaline* pumping music and rides.

Unfortunately, it also increases the risk-taking by young people. Young drivers are more likely to speed, drink and drive, not wear seatbelts and are four times more likely to die in a car accident. In a 2013 survey 41% of US teens reported being sexually active, with a massive three out of four of them not using contraception! The use of alcohol also increases risk taking by young people, with 58% of all males over 12 and 47% of all females being active drinkers. The Harvard report also shows that of those aged between 12-17 years old, 15% of boys and 14% girls report active drinking.

The teenage brain is doing what it can to seek pleasure or reward. Things like food, alcohol, drugs and sex all increase *dopamine* levels, so the young person will often throw themselves into activities involving one or more of them.

Again, Morgan explains three different theories for the length and emotional turbulence in puberty:

1. That human lives are so complex that we need a longer period of adolescence than other mammals.

2. That every generation's teenage life is more complex than the previous generations. Nevertheless, in reality they are influenced by the changing world around them. It is said that Socrates said, "The children now love luxury. They have bad manners, contempt for authority; they show disrespect for elders and love chatter in place of exercise."

3. That the teenage mind is seeking independence, whilst at the same time enjoy the benefits of being under the care of their parents (food, warmth, a bed, security).

Key points from this chapter

- Adolescence is a time for young people to form their independence from their parents.
- Puberty affects dopamine levels and this can lead to a reduction in feeling pleasure.
- Risk-taking increases during puberty.
- Adolescence is longer in humans than other mammals.
- The modern world is more complex than previous generations experienced.
- The teenage brain enjoys the security of their parents, whilst also seeking independence.

The Impact of Alcohol, Sex and Drugs

We briefly mentioned alcohol in the last section, but it is important that we cover it in more depth as alcohol misuse during this time can impair the development of the brain (Brown, Tapert, Granholm and Delis, 2000).

The *hippocampus* is the organ in the brain that helps to regulate emotions and help to store long-term memory. Research has shown that adolescents with alcohol disorders have significantly smaller left and right hippocampi (De Bellis et al., 2000). Swartzwelder, Wilson & Tayyeb (1995) found that it takes half the amount of alcohol to have a negative impact on this region in an immature brain compared to an adult brain.

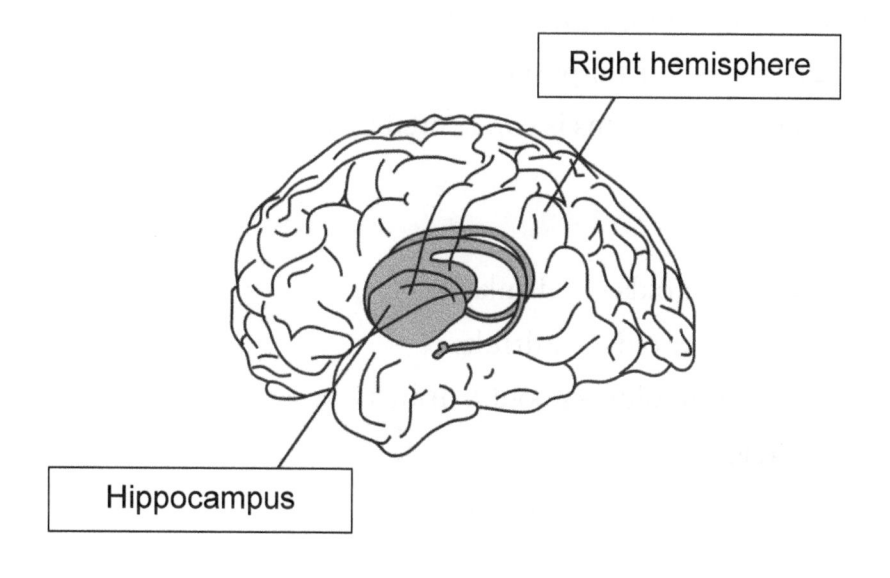

It is not just the brain that drinking alcohol during adolescence affects. It is estimated that about 40% of alcoholics started drinking between the ages of 15-19 (Helzeer, Burnam & McEvoy, 1991). According to the American Academy of Child and Adolescent Psychiatry 50% of accidental deaths in 15 to 24 year olds involve alcohol or drugs.

There are many factors that contribute to children drinking, such as peer pressure, culture, stress, anxiety or a need for independence. This can often lead to binge drinking, or 'getting drunk'.

The National Institute on Alcohol Abuse and Alcoholism in the USA report that a massive 11% of alcohol consumption in the country is by young people aged 12-20! They state that 90% of young people's consumption is through binge drinking, which in the different age groups is considered to be:

> **Boys**
> 9-13 year olds – 3 drinks
> 14-15 year olds – 4 drinks
> 16-17 year olds – about 5 drinks
> **Girls**
> 9-17 year olds – 3 drinks

Perception of the use of alcohol is a huge factor, the Department of Health in the UK identify that 71% of 15 and 16 year olds associate alcohol consumption with positive consequences and having fun. They estimate that there are approximately half a million children aged 11-15 who have been drunk in the last four weeks. Moreover, research shows that people who start drinking before the age of 15 are four times more likely to become alcohol dependent. It is therefore important that parents and adults around young people model safe and responsible drinking habits.

Another area of concern for many adults is the use of drugs by children. The NHS (2006) report that in England 4% of 11-15 year olds use Class A drugs (the most dangerous drugs, such as cocaine, LSD or ecstasy). Of the 11-16 year olds who had taken drugs, only 43% wanted to give it up immediately and 13% said they did not want to stop!

As with alcohol, it is important that adults are modelling a responsible attitude towards drugs. In the same report, the NHS report that nearly half of young people 14-16 years old have tried drugs, so it is highly likely that your child will encounter them. Rather than avoid the topic altogether, consider helping your child to be educated about them, so they can make informed choices.

Sex is another important part of the emerging young adult's life. During puberty, relationships tend to be more intense and fleeting. Not only do young people have to contend with relationship issues, they also have gender identity, sexuality and romantic identity to consider.

When it comes to gender, young people are identifying themselves with many different options, for example transgirl, transboy, gender fluid and at least thirteen other options. Sexuality choices for young people can include straight, gay, lesbian, homosexual, bisexual, asexual, polysexual and pansexual.

They are also separating out romantic identity, which represents a combination of gender identity and sexuality of the person they are seeking a relationship with. A far more complex situation than when we grew up.

In the most recent National Survey of Sexual Attitudes and Lifestyles (2010-2012), only 7.1% of males and 14.1% of females identified their parents as their main sources of information about sexual matters, whereas the overall number citing their school as the main source was a massive 40.3%. They found that about a third of 16-24 year olds had sexual intercourse before the age of sixteen. The survey showed that prior to their first sexual encounter young people wanted more information from their school and parents on mental or emotional attitudes to sex and about sexually transmitted infections.

There is obviously a great deal of stress and emotions related to the psychological side of this aspect of development, without thinking about the hormones flooding through their system. The growth in the cerebellum region of the brain can increase the stress a teen is under, and cause clumsiness for some.

For boys their body experiences an increase of *testosterone*, the sex hormone that triggers the development of the testes and prostate. The presence of this drug, which is elevated after physical exercise, increases aggressive behaviour. Morgan (2005) reports that even though boys are more likely to communicate their feelings, they feel emotions just as strongly.

For girls, they experience elevated levels of *oestrogen*, which increases the level of dopamine in the body and can cause mood swings.

Girls particularly, but also boys to some extent, have a subconscious drive that they have an imperfect body shape and they want to achieve an attractive figure. This is partially fed by the images seen in popular culture.

As we have discussed there are a huge number of factors that we now understand far more than we have in the past. Young people nowadays live in a different culture than when we grew up and are far more receptive to thinking about complex issues that were not discussed in the past. For further help or guidance on these conversations, my books *The Parent's Guide to the Modern World* and the self-read for teens *The Young Person's Guide to the Modern World* cover these topics in more depth.

Key points from this chapter

- Alcohol misuse during puberty affects the hippocampi.
- Drinking before the age of 15 increases the chance of becoming alcohol dependent.
- Nearly half of 14-16 year olds have tried drugs.
- Young people have to content with establishing their gender, romantic and sexual identity.
- Few young people turn to their parents for advice about these issues.
- Testosterone is elevated in boys and oestrogen is elevated in girls – both can cause emotional issues.
- There is a subconscious drive to achieve the perfect body.

A.W.O.L. the missing teenage brain

The impact on mental health

Scans of the brain during adolescence show that the cortex becomes thinner during puberty. The regions of the brain which undergo the most changes at this time are also the regions linked to mental health problems, such as depression and schizophrenia.

The prefrontal lobes, a region of the brain linked to controlling impulses does not mature until the early 20s. This has a huge impact on their ability to regulate emotions, increased impulsivity and more risk-taking – three risk factors for mental wellbeing. Difficulties with emotion regulation have been linked with the development of depression, substance use and eating disorders.

Immature prefrontal operation is also associated with more short-term decision-making. Particularly in the heat of the moment, they may struggle to see the long-term benefits and so make a decision that gives them immediate gains. Again, poor decision making is linked with mental health problems.

There is also an increased desire by teenagers to seek high intensity, exciting and arousing activities. Adrenaline pumping activities, like amusement parks, horror films, loud music, sex and drugs become very inviting.

Dopamine levels are also higher in the brain during puberty, than before or after. High levels of dopamine are linked to anxiety, hyperactivity, insomnia, mania, paranoia, stress and agitation.

Adolescent changes also predisposes young people to experience stress, especially during early puberty. Stress has a significant link with the development of most mental health problems.

Key points from this chapter

- The cortex gets thinner during puberty.
- The regions going through the most changes are linked to mental health problems.
- There are difficulties with emotional regulation, impulsivity and risk-taking.
- Elevated levels of dopamine can cause issues for teens.
- There is a link between mental health and stress, which is common during adolescence.

A.W.O.L. the missing teenage brain

Part Two
Mental Health Problems

A.W.O.L. the missing teenage brain

Common Mental Health Problems

In this chapter, we will cover an introduction to some of the common mental health problems that adolescents encounter. As I am sure you will be aware, there is a great deal of research and theory in the mental health domain, which it is hard to do justice to here in a brief few pages. Instead, the purpose of these pages is to introduce you to the various terms, conditions and theory, with each will signpost you to further sources of information.

I have included a description relating to some sections taken from the Diagnostic and Statistical Manual of Mental Disorders (known as the DSM). This is the accepted international standard relating to the diagnosis of mental health conditions. The purpose of this is not to alarm you, but to help raise your awareness of the full conditions. The more awareness people have of the worst-case scenario then the easier it is to recognise and act when a mental health problem is low-level and more likely to be turned round without interventions from doctors or other professionals.

A word of warning first – it is natural to read the symptoms of the various conditions and start to look for them in yourself or your child. Whilst I cannot stop your brain doing this, I would encourage you to refrain from doing the equivalent of diagnosis by internet. We cover what to do if you are concerned about your child and highlight common sources of support in the following part.

Finally, it is important to differentiate mental health difficulties with mental health problems. The use of the word difficulties in the former refers to the difficulties that everyone experiences at some point in their lives. It may be a period of stress, a relationship breakup or time of loss or grief. This is perfectly natural and the difficulties they are experiencing are part of the healing process. The support network people have at these times are vital in helping them to get over the difficulties and return to their normal state of wellbeing.

The use of the phrase mental health problems is more related to the onset of the conditions we will cover in the next few pages. The behaviours or symptoms you observe may be the early stages of a mental health condition, or they may not. Regardless, the important thing to understand is that if the sufferer does not have access to coping strategies or a good support network, then the impact can be far more severe. We will talk later about what some of these strategies can look like.

A.W.O.L. the missing teenage brain

Anxiety

> *Anxiety disorders include disorders that share features of excessive fear and anxiety and related behavioral disturbances. Fear is the emotional response to real or perceived imminent threat, whereas anxiety is anticipation of future threat. Obviously, these two states overlap, but they also differ, with fear more often associated with surges of autonomic arousal necessary for fight or flight, thoughts of immediate danger, and escape behaviors, and anxiety more often associated with muscle tension and vigilance in preparation for future danger and cautious or avoidant behaviors. Sometimes the level of fear or anxiety is reduced by pervasive avoidance behaviors. Panic attacks feature prominently within the anxiety disorders as a particular type of fear response. Panic attacks are not limited to anxiety disorders but rather can be seen in other mental disorders as well.*
>
> Diagnostic and Statistical Manual of Mental Disorders, 5th Edition

There are a number of conditions that can broadly be termed as anxiety-related. These include panic attacks, general anxiety, separation anxiety, phobias, and social anxiety. The next few pages will go through each of these.

Anxiety is caused by a perceived, imagined or real threat to the individual. There are a number of factors that contribute to the development of an anxiety disorder, such as a person's temperament, a family history of anxiety, life events, traumatic events, or even history of being in a strict environment where there is a fear of getting things wrong, feeling alone, insecure or confused.

Panic Attacks

Panic disorder has been frequently associated with *agoraphobia* – intense fear or anxiety in public, open spaces or crowds. Recently, this has become a separately diagnosable condition in its own right. Panic attacks are a key component of panic disorder. There are two types of panic attacks – expected and unexpected.

To be diagnosed with panic disorder a sufferer needs to experience regular panic attacks, which cannot be explained by any other reason (for example drugs, medication, another anxiety condition, phobia or OCD). They must be recurrent, often unexpected and be followed by at least a month of the person fearing they will reoccur and subsequent behaviour changes to attempt to avoid it reoccurring.

A panic attack is diagnosed with four or more of the following symptoms:

- Faster heart rate/palpitations,
- Sweating,
- Trembling/shaking,
- Short of breath or feeling of being smothered,
- A feeling of choking,
- Chest pain/discomfort,
- Nausea/Abdominal distress,
- Dizziness/unsteadiness/light headed/faint,
- Feeling of unreality or being detached from themselves,
- Fear of losing control/being crazy,
- Fear of dying,
- Numbness/tingling sensation,
- Chills/hot flushes.

General Anxiety

Someone who suffers with General Anxiety Disorder experiences anxiety over a long period about a wide range of situations or issues. They feel anxious or insecure most days and struggle to feel relaxed. The symptoms include feeling restless or worried, difficulty sleeping or concentrating, dizziness and heart palpitations.

Although it is not entirely clear what causes General Anxiety Disorder, the condition has been linked to a number of different things:

- Over activity of the emotion regions of the brain and the release of cortisol;
- An imbalance of the chemicals regulating mood;
- Difficulties in the attachment with their parents;
- Family history of the condition;
- Childhood experiences of overprotection or lack of emotional warmth;
- Neglect, abuse, trauma or stressful life events;
- A history of drug or alcohol abuse;
- A painful long-term health condition.

Separation Anxiety

Separation anxiety is used to describe fear and insecurity caused by separating from a particular person or people. There can be a number of reasons that this can cause overwhelming distress when a sufferer attempts to leave their home or a particular person. They may find it becomes all consuming, constantly worrying about the separation, refusing to leave the house or faking illnesses/finding reasons to avoid going to school/work.

During the first few years of life, humans learn to feel secure in themselves, their self-identity and their value as an individual. This happens through the process of attachment described early in this book. When things threaten or scare an infant, their parent's response helps limit their fear responses and establishes internal working models that continue into adulthood. This establishes the pattern of response to a particular threat, such as being reassured that when a parent leaves they will return.

However, this is only one possible contributing factor. A common factor is a history of trauma or an event that has made the sufferer feel insecure, such as the death of a loved one, an injury or house move. Another factor can be the anxiousness of parents, who then project this anxiety onto their children by being over-protective. Frequently there is a family history of anxiety.

Phobias

Fears are generally learned in three different ways – a direct experience, a socially learned fear or a combination of the both. Phobias, on the other hand, are an intense or irrational fear of a specific object or situation. These are divided up into four categories:

- Natural (e.g. lightening),
- Mutilation (e.g. dentist or injections),
- Animal (e.g. spiders),
- Situational (e.g. enclosed spaces).

To be diagnosed with a specific phobia, a person must:

- Have an unreasonable and excessive fear;
- Prompts an immediate anxiety response;
- Avoidance or extreme distress;
- The condition is life-limiting;
- It has lasted for over six months;
- Have symptoms not caused by another condition or disorder.

Social Anxiety

Someone who experiences discomfort in social situations, embarrassment and fear of being judged may be suffering with Social Anxiety Disorder or Social Phobia. This is different from someone who has an introvert personality. According to the DSM as many as 7% of children and adults in the US may be suffering from the disorder. A massive 75% of those diagnosed with Social Anxiety Disorder began experiencing the symptoms between the ages of 8 to 15.

The criteria for diagnosis are:

- Fear or anxiety related to social situations;
- Fear of showing their anxiety and experiencing social rejection;
- Consistent distress caused by social situations;
- Avoidance or painful endurance of social situations;
- Disproportionate fear and anxiety for the situation;
- Ongoing for more than six months;
- Cause personal distress and impaired functioning in an area of their lives (for example their work);
- It is not related to another condition or disorder;

- If there is a condition that could cause self-consciousness (such as eczema or a scar), then the fear and anxiety are disproportionate.

Because of the nature of the disorder, it can be confused with similar conditions, such as agoraphobia, general anxiety disorder, post-traumatic stress disorder or depression. It may also be confused with someone who is an introvert, shy or even on the autistic spectrum.

Common Mental Health Problems

Key points from this chapter

- Panic attacks can be expected or unexpected.
- General Anxiety Disorder describes someone who experiences anxiety all or most of the time.
- Separation anxiety describes someone who experiences anxiety when separated from a particular person or people.
- Phobias are learned, derived from an experience or a combination of both.
- Social anxiety describes someone who experiences discomfort, embarrassment or fear of being judged in social situations.

A.W.O.L. the missing teenage brain

Obsessive-Compulsive Disorders

The essential feature of this disorder is recurrent obsessional thoughts or compulsive acts... Obsessional thoughts are ideas, images or impulses that enter the individual's mind again and again in a stereotyped form. They are almost invariably distressing (because they are violent or obscene, or simply because they are perceived as senseless) and the sufferer often tries, unsuccessfully, to resist them. They are, however, recognized as the individual's own thoughts, even though they are involuntary and often repugnant. Compulsive acts or rituals are stereotyped behaviours that are repeated again and again. They are not inherently enjoyable, nor do they result in the completion of inherently useful tasks... anxiety symptoms are often present, but distressing feelings of internal or psychic tension without obvious autonomic arousal are also common. There is a close relationship between obsessional symptoms, particularly obsessional thoughts, and depression...

The International Classification of Diseases

In the last few years, there has been much more understanding of Obsessive-Compulsive Disorders (or OCD), although scientists are a long way from fully understanding it. It affects both men and women equally; symptoms often begin in males during late adolescence and in females during their early twenties.

For many years, it was widely thought that OCD was a learned condition, brought on by the environment, stress and parental styles. To be clear, there is currently no evidence backing up these claims. Instead, there are a number of theories on what could contribute to the development of OCD:

- Genes – there are various views around the world that because OCD often runs in families that there is a genetic link. However, that does not explain identical twins, where one develops OCD and the other does not.

- The brain – it is normal for the brain to have a drive for certain actions, such as washing dirty hands. Once we perform that action, this drive subsides. The theory is that something about the make-up of this circuit is broken or interrupted.

- Serotonin – this is a hormone that helps to send messages between the cells in the brain and regulating things like anxiety. There is one view that sufferers may have abnormal levels or an imbalance.

- Depression – this is closely linked to the condition, but there are split views on whether it could cause OCD or whether it is caused by the condition.

- Illness or infections during childhood – severe infections can precede symptoms of OCD, but it is believed that sufferers are predisposed to have the condition already.

- Life events or trauma – these may happen just before the onset of OCD, however, it is felt that those sufferers were predisposed to it.

OCD is a condition where the sufferer experiences unwanted and unpleasant thoughts about something (for example germs or electrical fire), which causes anxiety, disgust or unease. To alleviate these decisions, the individual will then use repetitive behaviour or mental acts to try to stop the unpleasant thoughts for a short time.

Treatment may consist of drug therapies to address chemical imbalances in the brain or cognitive behavioural therapy (CBT) to address the thought patterns.

Common Mental Health Problems

Key points from this chapter

- Obsessive Compulsive Disorder describes recurrent obsessive thoughts or compulsive actions.
- These can be intrusive or unwarranted for the sufferer.
- It may be caused by a combination of genetics, an issue in the brain, altered serotonin levels, depression, illness or infections, or traumatic event(s).
- Treatment will involve helping the sufferer to manage the thought patterns.

A.W.O.L. the missing teenage brain

Eating Disorders

> *Feeding and eating disorders are characterized by a persistent disturbance of eating or eating-related behavior that results in the altered consumption or absorption of food and that significantly impairs physical health or psychosocial functioning. Diagnostic criteria are provided for pica, rumination disorder, avoidant/restrictive food intake disorder, anorexia nervosa, bulimia nervosa, and binge-eating disorder.*
>
> Diagnostic and Statistical Manual of Mental Disorders, 5th Edition

Most sufferers of eating disorders are female, most commonly young women from 13 to 17 years old. There are three types of common eating disorders: *Anorexia Nervosa, Bulimia* and *Binge Eating Disorder*. When symptoms do not match these then professionals may diagnose a person with an *Other Specified Feeding or Eating Disorder*. It is not clear what causes eating disorders at the moment, people are more likely to experience them if there is a history of family eating disorders, they have been criticised for their eating habits, and they have anxiety, have been sexually abused, are concerned with being slim or have an obsessive personality.

Anorexia Nervosa

This condition is characterised by an inaccurate perception of their own body image or body weight. The sufferer will often restrict their diet or overly exercise in order to try to achieve the 'perfect' body weight.

Sufferers will often control the intake of foods they see as fattening, may take appetite suppressants, make themselves sick, take laxatives or exercise excessively. In turn, this can cause physical problems, such as dizziness, hair loss, dry skin or absence of periods.

Unfortunately, anorexia can lead to serious problems or even death. The NHS in England identify that anorexia is one of the most common causes of death related to mental health problems, whether it be from physical complications or suicide. Other related problems, caused by the impact to the body, can include kidney, muscle and bone problems, fertility issues, heart and circulation issues, fits, loss of concentration or memory, bowel problems or a weakened immune system.

Fortunately, sufferers can overcome anorexia. It can take time and will involve a therapeutic input, which may include CBT.

Bulimia

Bulimia sufferers will experience cycles, going through periods of binge-eating and then a purging period, where they make themselves sick, take laxatives or undertake excessive exercise to try and stop them gaining weight. Bulimia can be referred to as a 'hidden' eating disorder. Sufferers may hide their behaviour and because of this cycle, the sufferer may not appear over or under weight.

Side effects of bulimia can include tiredness, weakness, problems with periods, dental problems, dry skin, brittle fingernails, swollen glands, fits, bone problems, heart, kidney or even bowel problems (such as constipation). People overcome bulimia, it takes time and will likely involve therapy, such as CBT.

Binge Eating Disorder

Unlike Bulimia, Binge Eating Disorder purely consists of excessive food intake in a short period of time. This may be on impulse, or it may be planned – including buying the food in advance. The sufferer may put on weight, but not all the time, or may hide how much they are eating. Treatment may involve self-help guides or therapies, such as CBT.

Key points from this chapter

- Anorexia sufferers have an inaccurate perception of their weight or their body shape.
- They will control their intake of food, may excessively exercise, or take laxatives, appetite suppressants or make themselves vomit.
- Anorexia can lead to death.
- Anorexia can be overcome.
- Bulimia is often hidden as they mask the behaviour or maintain their body weight.
- Bulimia sufferers will have a cycle of binge-eating and expulsion.
- Someone suffering with Binge Eating Disorder will go through phases of over eating, this may be planned or unplanned.

A.W.O.L. the missing teenage brain

Depression

> *Depressive disorders include disruptive mood dysregulation disorder, major depressive disorder (including major depressive episode), persistent depressive disorder (dysthymia), premenstrual dysphoric disorder, substance/medication-induced depressive disorder, depressive disorder due to another medical condition, other specified depressive disorder, and unspecified depressive disorder... The common feature of all of these disorders is the presence of sad, empty, or irritable mood, accompanied by somatic and cognitive changes that significantly affect the individual's capacity to function. What differs among them are issues of duration, timing, or presumed [cause].*
>
> Diagnostic and Statistical Manual of Mental Disorders, 5th Edition

There are two categories of depression, those, which meet the criteria for diagnosis of Major Depressive Disorder, and those, which do not. Those that do not are often short-term in nature, potentially caused by stress or environmental factors. As these factors change and the person learns different coping mechanisms, the depression subsides.

Major Depressive Disorders have a long-term impact on a person's life. There are times that they are diagnosed with some extra wording:

> *With Anxious Distress* – reflects the additional complexity of anxiety combined with depression;

> *With Mixed Features* – allows for diagnosis of one of the types of depression without meeting the full criteria.

According to Bailey and Shooter (2009) 1-2% of children, 4-5% of adolescents are suffering with depression and there are known links with a family history of depression.

For children, Major Depressive Disorder include:

Disruptive Mood Dysregulation Disorder

This was recently added to the diagnostic manual for mental health conditions for 6 to 18 year olds in order to reduce the amount of adolescent bipolar diagnoses. It describes someone who is irritable or angry most of every day; has severe temper outbursts (3+ per week) over and above their temperament; and has trouble functioning in more than one environment (e.g.

school, home). To be diagnosed someone has to have experienced symptoms for more than 12 months.

Premenstrual Dysphoric Disorder (PMDD)

This condition is used to describe someone who, for the two weeks prior to a period, experiences severe emotional symptoms (depression, angry outbursts, irritability, anxiety, confusion, social withdrawal) or physical symptoms (breast tenderness, abdominal bloating, headache or swelling of extremities).

Persistent Depressive Disorder (PDD)

The sufferer experiences episodes of major depression, with periods of less severe symptoms over at least two years.

Psychotic Depression

A combination of a form of depression with psychosis – for example delusions, seeing or hearing things.

Seasonal Affective Disorder

Someone who experiences the onset of depression during winter months.

Bipolar Disorder

This can be referred to as manic depression, but is not technically a form of depression. This condition is characterised by a cycle of abnormally high-elevated moods (the manic phase), with severe depressive periods (depression phase). Sufferers will often experience extreme reactions to life's difficulties. The condition runs in families and tends to be diagnosed in the later teenage years or early 20s.

In their manic period, sufferers experience periods of busyness or high levels of activity. They may take big risks, not stop themselves and even be promiscuous. Bipolar Disorder can lead to symptoms of delusions consistent with psychosis. The periods of depression will often build up over time.

Key points from this chapter

- Depression is split into two types – a Major Depressive Disorder or depression not linked to a Major Depressive Disorder.
- Depression may be diagnosed with associated anxiety problems, or with mixed features.
- Disruptive Mood Dysregulation Disorder is a condition diagnosed in 6-18 year olds who have severe anger outbursts and is irritable or angry most of the time.
- Someone who has Premenstrual Dysphoric Disorder experiences symptoms for the two weeks leading up to their period.
- Persistent Depressive Disorder describes someone with major depressive symptoms for more than two years.
- Psychotic Depression describes someone who has depression combined with psychosis.
- Seasonal Affective Disorder is a seasonal depressive condition, normally throughout the winter months.
- Bipolar Disorder is not a form of depression. Sufferers experience phases of mania and also depression.

A.W.O.L. the missing teenage brain

Psychosis

> *Schizophrenia spectrum and other psychotic disorders include schizophrenia, other psychotic disorders, and schizotypal (personality) disorder. They are defined by abnormalities in one or more of the following five domains: delusions, hallucinations, disorganized thinking (speech), grossly disorganized or abnormal motor behavior (including catatonia), and negative symptoms.*
>
> Diagnostic and Statistical Manual of Mental Disorders, 5th Edition

Very simply the brain responds the same way for things people imagine as it does for things they experience. If they fear snakes, then imagining them can cause just as much anxiety, fear and stress as if they were actually in their presence. Now, consider hallucinations, whether they are imagined sounds, sights, touch or taste. Imagine not being able to tell the difference between imagined things and reality. Imagine not even knowing that the things you are seeing or hearing are not real. It is estimated in Bailey and Shooter (2009, p265) that about 1 in 200 young people experience psychosis at any one time, although a review by Kelleher et al (2012) found that on average 17% of 9-12 year olds reported hearing voices or sounds that others could not hear and 7.5% of 13-18 years old reported the same.

Psychosis, whatever the cause, is characterised by hallucinations and it can be hard for sufferers to tell the difference between them and reality, or in serious cases lose touch with reality as they engage more with the hallucinations.

There are positive and negative symptoms associated with psychosis. The positive symptoms are things that appear in the sufferer's life (they are added), such as seeing things that are not there, hearing voices, racing thoughts or delusions. Negative symptoms are things they stop doing, such as eating regularly, reduction in socialising, apathy or caring for their own wellbeing and self-hygiene. There is also an emotional impact, with negative symptoms including a possible reduction in the range or intensity of emotions – almost a lack of emotion. Negative symptoms can occur up to 12 months before the onset of the positive symptoms. Cognitive symptoms can also occur, such as difficulty concentrating, with remembering things, following instructions, understanding things or expressing themselves.

Psychosis can be caused by a number of different things, including:

- Alcohol or drug abuse;
- Lack of sleep;
- Stress;
- Anxiety;
- Major depression;
- Low blood sugar;
- Fever;
- Medical conditions, such as a brain tumour or multiple sclerosis,;
- Bipolar disorder;
- Schizophrenia.

Schizophrenia

Schizophrenia is thought to affect about 1% of the population. It is a mental disorder that affects how someone thinks, feels and behaves. It is typically characterised by psychosis for a period of time. The cause of schizophrenia is unknown, although there may be links to someone's DNA or long-term cannabis use. There is no current cure for the condition; however, the symptoms can be managed through therapy, such as CBT and medication.

The onset of schizophrenia typically begins between the ages of 15 and 35. For males, it is most common from 16 years to 25; for women it is most common over the age of 30.

Key points from this chapter

- Hallucinations consist of a sufferer responding to imaginary senses.
- Psychosis involves a combination of symptoms added into someone's life (hallucinations and delusions) and negative symptoms (such as lack of regular eating, socialising and self-care).
- There are many causes of psychosis.
- Schizophrenia is one cause of psychosis and is thought to affect 1% of the population.
- The cause of schizophrenia is unknown, it can run in families and also can be linked to drug use.

A.W.O.L. the missing teenage brain

Self-harm

Deliberate self-harm is identified in the Diagnostic and Statistical Manual of Mental Disorders, 5th Edition as the act of intentionally hurting themselves or putting themselves at risk in order to either get relief from negative feelings or cognitive state, to resolve a interpersonal issue or finally to induce a feeling of positivity. To be diagnosed someone must have deliberately self-inflicted injuries, without an intention to commit suicide, on at least five days in the course of a year.

Sufferers will often feel a release or relief during the act (as though they deserve it) or afterwards (it is a release), and their behaviour may indicate over time that they are dependent on repeating this behaviour.

Deliberate self-harm can take several forms:

- Poisoning;
- Cutting, hitting, burning;
- Picking or pulling skin/hair;
- Self-strangulation;
- Sexual promiscuity;
- Alcohol/drug misuse.

Self-harm excludes acts like picking a scab, nail-biting, tattooing, body piercing or other culturally acceptable behaviours. Deliberate self-harm excludes behaviours displayed during times of other mental disorders, psychosis or drug or alcohol intoxication or withdrawal.

The sufferer will often have friendship or family issues, insecurity, anxiety, depression or stress. Many will find their mind uncontrollably preoccupied with the self-harm, even if they are not acting on it, for days or weeks. That said, many young people who self-harm for the first time do it on impulse, Bailey & Shooter (2009, p287) identify that this might be as short as 15 minutes before carrying out the act. They state that only 20% of adolescents have tried self-harming before.

Self-harm is almost certainly linked to a lack of available support networks for whatever the sufferer is facing – if they had the ability to seek the support from their wider network or express it, and then it would take away the need to self-harm. There may be a family history of self-harm or they may have experienced abuse. The Royal College of Psychiatrists in the UK identify that about 10% of young people will try self-harming at some point. Treatments may include self-help advice, group or family therapy or interventions, such as CBT.

Suicide

Suicide is the leading non-accidental cause of death in young people, Young Minds in the UK identify that nearly 25% of young people will feel suicidal at some point. Male teens are less likely than females to get support for depression and four times as likely to kill themselves as females. They are also less likely to call for help. On the other hand, female young people are more likely to attempt to kill themselves.

The phrase 'commit' suicide relates back to the times when it was an illegal act. Nowadays, it is more common to take about people killing themselves, died by suicide or completed suicide.

There is one theory that the changes in the brain described earlier, especially the pre-frontal cortex, could explain why so many young people feel forced to attempt to take their own lives when overwhelmed.

If someone if planning to try to kill themselves, then they are likely to:

- Plan it;
- Make preparations;

- Hide any evidence of self-harm (if they have been);
- Work out how not to be discovered;
- Joke about it with others;
- Write a suicide note.

Key points from this chapter

- Self-harm is the act of hurting themselves in order to self-punish or provide relief from their negative feelings or thoughts.
- There are different forms of self-harm:
    - Poisoning;
    - Cutting, hitting, burning;
    - Picking or pulling skin/hair;
    - Self-strangulation;
    - Sexual promiscuity;
    - Alcohol/drug misuse.
- Self-harm is linked to the lack of a support network the sufferer feels they can access for support.
- Many young people do not plan to self-harm and may only consider it 15 minutes before they do it.
- Females are more likely to attempt suicide as a call for help.
- Males are more likely to die by suicide.
- Someone thinking about suicide may show planning activities.

A.W.O.L. the missing teenage brain

Chronic Fatigue Syndrome

This controversial condition is also known as Myalgic Encephalopathy or ME. For many years health organisations did not think it existed in its own right. It is now estimated that as many as 0.4% of the population, including children, suffer with ME.

With this condition, a small amount of physical exertion can lead to severe physical symptoms, such as a short walk leading to needing to rest for several hours or days. Ultimately, the condition can lead to someone becoming bed-bound or developing muscle fatigue.

Symptoms are similar to both anxiety and depression, so it is included in this text, as these will both be considered prior to consideration of ME. The causes of it are unknown and sufferers experience poor physical health, combined with physical symptoms that lead to a substantial impairment. Treatment is often managed through self-help or talking therapies.

Key points from this chapter

- Chronic Fatigue Syndrome has recently been established as a recognised condition.
- Physical exertion can lead to an exaggerated amount of pain or tiredness.
- Symptoms are similar to anxiety and depression.

Loss and Grief

The loss of someone close to a young person, whether through death or separation, can have a profound effect on them. The normal grief process is to be expected in all children (subject to their age, see below). However, for some young people, loss or grief can have a far more long-term impact.

Unfortunately, for some children, the grieving process or difficulties with their support network can cause psychosomatic (body and mind) problems. This might include:

- Anxiety;
- Breathing problems;
- Chest pains;
- Chronic pain syndrome;
- Conversion disorder (historically known as hysteria);
- Depression;
- Headaches;
- Hypochondria;
- Insomnia;
- Loss of appetite;
- Painful periods.

How the concept of loss and grief normally develops (from Bailey & Shooter, 2009, Christ, 2000 and Willis, 2002):

Age (years)	Concept of death	Grief
0-2	Very little.	Likely to cry at separation. Respond to the emotions of those around them.
3-5	Will see death as temporary. May feel they caused it.	May ask questions. Feel overwhelmed when exposed to adults' grief. Dislike changes in routine. May develop fear of abandonment or separation.
6-8	Understand the finality of death.	May join in with 'grief' behaviours, but forgotten quickly. Better express emotions and

		feelings, such as anger, fear or sadness. Behaviour may regress. May speak about wanting to die to be with lost ones.
9-11	Require factual information about the death.	May avoid strong or intense emotions in themselves or others who are grieving. May want to be seen as 'strong'.
12-14	Avoid talking about it. May express disbelief. Development of spiritual beliefs about where they have gone.	May express anger or distain. Preoccupied about public emotional control.

| 15-17 | Understand the permanence of death. | More like the grief of adults, but shorter in duration Interfere with normal daily functioning. Not able to be controlled by immersion into activities. Externalising behaviours (drinking, arguments, anger, testing limits). |

Key points from this chapter

- Grief after a loss is natural.
- During adolescence there may be difficulties with this process, particularly is they feel they do not have access to support.
- The concept of death and grieving process is different at different ages.

A.W.O.L. the missing teenage brain

What to do if you are Concerned

If you are concerned about the mental health of a young person, then it is important that you seek early help from a mental health professional. Many professionals will refer to this as the point at which it is having an impact on the quality of their daily life. Most support is accessed through the young person's doctor as the first point of call, although they may also be accessed through other professionals, such as the school nurse or counsellor.

The signs that a young person needs help are a combination of:

- Sleeping more than usual;
- Refusal to get out of bed;
- Spending more time alone than before;

- Finding it hard to handle a situation and it becoming mind consuming;
- Eating patterns change;
- Upset over a long period of time;
- Difficulty concentrating;
- Getting angry or aggressive quickly;
- Moaning about aches in their body;
- Disengaged with people, friends and school work;
- Low mood;
- Anxiety;
- Tearfulness;
- Not doing so well at school;
- Not doing the activities they used to enjoy;
- Ignoring phone calls from friends;
- Turning down invitations from friends.

A long-term study of suicidal adolescents going into adult mental health services found that higher levels of parental support often meant that there were lower levels of depression reported, a lower likelihood of attempted suicide and less likelihood of using adult mental health services.

Possible treatments

There are many different forms of treatment a mental health professional will consider. They will often consider low-level interventions first, although for more serious cases, they may recommend a combination of different interventions.

Self-help

A young person may be given advice or strategies to help manage the condition themselves. This can include training them to look for early warning signs, how to use their support networks, keeping mood diaries, studying coping strategies or building self-esteem

Support networks

A vital element of feeling valued and confident is to have a good peer and adult support network. Those with a large support network, fewer negative relationships and access to people to seek support from are less likely to experience longer-term issues.

CBT

Cognitive Behaviour Therapy is based around the concept that by changing one of the factors affecting how someone thinks or reacts to something will change the way they respond. This talking therapy will focus on the sufferer's thoughts, beliefs, feelings and behaviours in order to change one of them and develop better coping strategies.

Counselling

Often one of the earliest intervention offered, counselling focusses on teaching someone coping strategies for the issue they are facing (it is top down, or problem orientated).

Other Talking Therapies

There are many other talking therapies available, such as art, drama or music therapy; family or group therapy are others often used. Therapy, unlike counselling, will often seek to identify where the issue is coming from and help a sufferer to address these issues.

Medication

For some mental health problems, medication or drug therapy has been shown to be effective. Some will seek to restore the chemical balance within the brain or body, whereas others act as symptom suppressors, allowing the individual to develop coping mechanisms.

Key points from this chapter

- Parental support is important for young people experiencing mental health difficulties.
- If you are concerned, seek early help from a mental health professional.
- Support is often accessed through a school counsellor or a young person's doctor.
- There are a number of different interventions that may be used on their own or in a combination.

What to do if you are Concerned

A.W.O.L. the missing teenage brain

Part Three
Other Factors Affecting Mental Wellbeing

A.W.O.L. the missing teenage brain

Self-Security and Trust

The biggest single most important thing to being able to cope with the challenges life brings is for your child to know their own identity, feel secure and to trust themselves.

This applies from their childhood through to old age. There are various theories about the development of self-identity and in turn, self-security. The way people bond with their parents as babies establishes a secure attachment with them, this teaches them that they are worthwhile individuals and that their needs will be met. These early beginnings form the basis of what eventually becomes their self-security.

This is not to say that early parenting has to be perfect. Professionals use a phrase called 'good enough' parenting to describe how, even when things are not textbook there are enough protective factors, or good things, in a baby's life to mean that they become secure. This was described by the English paediatrician and psychoanalyst, Winnicott, as 'holding', which is the process that parents go through by providing completely for their infant's needs to begin with and letting go gradually over time. Bion, a British psychoanalyst then extended this to describe what happens when a baby cries or is overwhelmed. At those times they often project their feelings onto their parents, who normally then limit or 'contain' the emotional overwhelm and calm the baby down. This 'containment' then teaches them how to limit their own overwhelm later in life.

This external regulation by an infant's parents teach it a sense of trust in the world. They learn that they can trust others to keep them safe, to look after them and meet their needs (such as feeding them when they are hungry). As they develop throughout their childhood and into adolescence, they become more self-sufficient – they develop trust in their own abilities to meet their own needs, they feel less of a need to rely on others. Because they know what trust feels like, as their social skills develop, they begin to recognise others they can trust. It will start with familiar adults, such as childminders or family, but then extend until, by teenage years, young people can recognise peers, friends and adults who they can trust with different aspects of their lives.

Whenever people feel insecure, feel they cannot trust others, or feel threatened in some way, psychologically they will seek 'containment' and often like to retreat to this inner safe place. For some people they like to have a 'duvet day', others like to have a hot bubble bath, some like their favourite foods – everyone has different ways of accessing their secure base. This makes them feel that everything is going to be alright and recharges them. Very often, people will say how much better they felt for doing nothing, when in actual fact what they were doing was containing their emotional overwhelm (for example stress).

Unfortunately, there are unsafe ways of getting this feeling too – sex, drugs and alcohol. These numb the brain and make it feel like a person is secure, even when they are not. Then when they come down, the insecurity is still there and so they seek the same numbness. Think of someone you know who drinks to forget, they feel alright when they are drinking, but when they sober up the pain is still there, so they mentally begin counting down the hours until they can drink again to take it away – the underlying threat has not been addressed and it won't be if the cycle continues.

Children are going to come across challenges in their life that challenge their self-security. Life is hard at times, it is easy to lose focus and beat themselves up about something. This can be even more so if they regret an action they did at the time, even if they thought it was the right things to and they learnt that it was not.

When they are challenged or they have experienced a tough day they need to know how to process and unwind in a safe, secure way without needing to turn to drugs, drink or sex. Unfortunately, society has set the expectation that when you have had a bad day, you have a drink. Make a decision about whether this is an expectation you want your child to learn. Teach them to use things like comfort food, a favourite TV programme, music, having a bubble bath or snuggling on the sofa. This escape or switching off from the world helps give them brain time to process the day and subconsciously reminds them of the security they felt when they were babies.

It is important that young people grow up being comfortable in their own skins and there will be times you have to support your child to accept the bits about them they cannot change and help them to change the parts they can work on. They should see the parts of their body and personality as part of their journey through life. It is part of who they are and sometimes, like events in the past, cannot be changed.

Body shape is not only controlled by diet and exercise, genetics plays a large part too. More than 400 scientists around the world came together in the years leading up to 2010 to investigate the links between genetics and body fat distribution. They found that someone's genes affect whether they are likely to be apple shaped (fatter around the waist) or pear-shaped (more fat in the thighs and bums). The genetic link was shown to have a larger impact in women. Therefore, whilst people can control their diet and exercise patterns, they may not have full control over their body shape anyway. The same applies with muscles; scientists have found evidence of 'muscular' genes that mean for some people it is easier to keep fit.

Self-security and self-identity is huge for children, they face so many pressures from within, let alone considering external pressures.

One thing that is likely to challenge their self-identity is their social life. It might be that they said or did something that upset others. It may be that someone else's actions or behaviours have upset them or made them feel insecure. Adolescents can be incredibly cruel at times.

Key points from this chapter

- It is important that we help young people to feel secure about themselves and to be able to trust others.
- This is developed in early life and re-accessed through a number of different activities.
- It is important that young people recognise how to access their secure-self to help deal with challenges they will encounter during life.
- There are unsafe ways of getting this feeling of security, such as drink, drugs or sex.
- Self-security can include being comfortable with their body shape.
- That genetics form part of a person's body shape and cannot be controlled by diet or exercise.

A.W.O.L. the missing teenage brain

Recognising Emotions

It is my belief that if the human race were more adept at recognising their emotions, then there would be far less conflict in the world.

When someone experience an emotion, several things happen. The emotion is often triggered by the brain reacting to something happening around them – a threat or praise for example. This can be something they are aware of, for example, praise is easy to spot, whereas with threats, they may not have even noticed them, but at an unconscious level the brain reacts.

Every person's brain reacts differently to external triggers – the way one person emotionally reacts to remembering a deceased relative will be different from another family member. Factors such as memories and previous experience; what else is going on; other people's emotions; culture; or even internal considerations like anxiety or depression.

At a basic level, emotions work like this. The *thalamus* receives the information from the senses (a sound or seeing something). This triggers the *hypothalamus* to release hormones. Other areas of the middle part of the brain (including the *hippocampus* and the *amygdala*) refer to memories to assess the information and decide how to react. This is known as the *limbic system*.

Sometimes the *limbic system* decides there is nothing to worry about and so tempers the emotional reaction. Other times, the signal is passed to the *frontal lobes*, who in turn decide how to react. For example, sometimes people react with anger to someone pushing in in front of them (a *limbic system* response) and other times they let it go (a *frontal lobe* response).

The process in the brain triggers the release of hormones throughout the body. In case of threat, the *sympathetic nervous system* automatically releases the hormones, such as *adrenaline*, to prepare the body for the fight, flight or freeze response. To potentially make matters worse, the HeartMath Institute, have found evidence that the heart is intuitive and can begin to react even before seeing a stimulus (such as a picture of a snake). These reactions in the body may happen even when the brain has tempered the reaction of the limbic system – ever decided to ignore something that could have angered you, but your body still feels tense or hot?

The key to recognising emotions is to learn to recognise how the body feels just before the brain kicks in. For example, pride will often be felt in the chest, worry in the stomach or anger in the hands or feet. By learning to act on these early warning signs, people become more emotionally literate over time – they read their emotions better and can then decide on an appropriate response.

Now, unfortunately, this is a skill that many do not have and during the turbulent teenage years, it is easy to be caught up in the reaction to the hormones, without the thought process that goes alongside it.

If you are concerned about this happening often in your child's life, then you could have a conversation with them about how your body feels at the early stages of your emotions and what you do to stop yourself from overreacting. Helping them to understand how you cope with your emotions when you feel them begin will model to them the sorts of choices they have. For example with some emotions people leave the room (changing the environment), for others it's going for a walk, phoning a friend, finding someone for a hug, doing an activity like a jigsaw, playing a game on their tablet, even breathing exercises or even repetitive physical exercise.

Key points from this chapter

- The brain reacts to incoming information, triggering the emotion.
- Emotional reactions are affected by a number of different experiences, the context, their culture, other people's emotions and conditions they suffer from.
- The limbic system will trigger the emotional response.
- Sometimes the cortex can decide an alternative emotion.
- The body's automated system will respond to the emotion, sometimes even if the cortex has overruled the emotional response.
- It is important that people recognise how their body feels and relate it to an emotional response.

A.W.O.L. the missing teenage brain

Coping with Emotions

With so many emotional changes going on in a day when your child feels happy help them to celebrate and when they feel sad help them to think about what is making them sad and moving on from the emotion. Get them to consider if is it something they have done or if they have they chosen to feel that way, an example would be when people let something minor spoil their day rather than shrug it off.

Emotions are temporary and people can often control how they feel. If we take the previous example of someone cutting in front of a car in a queue of traffic. Sometimes it makes the driver cross and they gesture or beep the horn; other times they let them in with a friendly gesture. Either way, this one incident does not normally affect their mood, it is the other way round, their mood affects the way they react to these events. If they take charge of their mood (for example by watching a comedy or playing some of their favourite music) then they can often revitalise themselves.

Music can have a profound effect on mood and is used by some as a coping mechanism. Saarikallio and Erkkilä (p96, 2007) reviewed the ways adolescents regulate their mood using music:

Regulatory function	Typical mood before	Typical mood after
Entertainment	Nothing specific, sometimes boredom.	Lifted spirits, maintaining positive mood.
Revival	Stress and treadmill, need for energy or relaxation.	Revival, relaxing and getting energy.
Strong sensation	No specific mood.	Intensity and attention become stronger.
Diversion	Anger, sadness, stress, 'depression' and annoying thoughts.	Forgetting about negative mood.

Discharge	Anger, sadness and 'depression'.	Expression of their current mood.
Mental work	Things that need thinking.	Imagery, insights, clarification and reappraisal of experiences.
Solace	Sad or troubled.	Feeling comforted or understood.

There will be many things that cause your child to experience strong emotions. The hormones that push their brain through puberty can send the emotional centre into overload. Combined with the shutting down of the higher brain areas, which usually help inhibit extreme emotions, it is not uncommon for the adolescent brain to feel overloaded. However, it is a temporary feeling – it is vital that your child recognises this and recognises things they can do to get themselves out of that temporary feeling. Help them to recognise the ways they can lift their mood, but also help them to have the vocabulary to be able to talk about how they feel.

Key points from this chapter

- Emotions are temporary, they do not have to set the thermometer for a whole day.
- There are multiple ways of changing an emotional mood.
- Adolescents will use music to regulate their mood.
- They will experience strong emotions and may feel overwhelmed at times.

Coping with Emotions

A.W.O.L. the missing teenage brain

Coping with Stress

Young people can often get stressed about academic work – remembering everything they need to, revising for exams, doing homework, learning to manage priorities, juggling academic demands with the demands being placed on them by their friends and family, even just managing their time can be a huge form of stress. For teenagers, parents are another common form of stress, with the adolescent trying to break free from their parents, whilst needing their almost constant support on a day-to-day basis.

Siblings can add an extra stress to their lives. Chandra and Batada (2006) found that 64% of the adolescents they interviewed reported worry about the stress caused by younger siblings. For the younger child this could be related to their desire to be more 'mature' and so for the older sibling captures the desire to distance themselves from their sibling, finding them 'annoying'. Same-aged or older siblings may also see their growing younger sibling as a threat. They, in turn, may be jealous of the independence that older siblings may have, whilst they still have to attend school, do homework and stick to curfews.

The other two causes of stress for adolescents are their social lives and romantic relationships. As we have already discussed, a teen's social life goes through a number of changes as they move from primary education to secondary education. Peer pressure is immense for young people going through puberty and the desire to find safety and fit into social groups can be overwhelming. The opposite end of the peer pressure spectrum is the young person who isolates himself or herself and hides away from social interaction and relationships. As we will discuss later, someone's support network is one of the biggest factors in helping them to avoid the impact of mental health difficulties.

Finally, for many of young people, adolescence is a time when they start to experiment with romantic relationships. As you may recall yourself, this can be an incredibly stressful experience. The 21st Century has brought a huge openness in terms of sexual, romantic and gender identify. However, technology and social media has also had a huge impact on this – those early romance baby steps being made more complex by the ability to be able to send or receive messages at any time, see whether someone has received them and even if they are typing a reply. Those replies, which in the past would have been more considered, are nowadays based on instant emotional reactions. It is no wonder so many young people find these early steps stressful.

High levels of stress over time have a negative effect on the body. When someone is stressed, the hormone *cortisol* is released. If the stress-response system is over stimulated for long periods of time, then it starts to have an impact on the body's systems. Heightened levels of stress can have an academic impact too – if someone is stressed, the brain is less likely to transfer learning into the memory.

Symptoms of long-term stress include:

- Weight gain,
- Sleep problems,
- Anxiety,
- Depression,

- Digestion problems,
- Headaches,
- Memory impairment,
- Concentration issues.

If they are feeling stressed, then there are proactive steps they can do to reduce that pressure. These often involve doing things that take their mind off the situation. Young people may benefit from some support with learning what is the best thing to do to help reduce their cortisol levels and help them to clear their head. By learning to do this, they will have more space to understand how to resolve the issues. Here are a few things they could try:

- Go for a walk;
- Go for a run;
- Stroke or care for a pet;
- Go out with friends;
- Phone up someone for a chat;
- Do some breathing exercises;
- Meditate;
- Practice Mindfulness;
- Perform Gratitude.

Long-term, there are several strategies to help avoid the build-up of stress. Many of the strategies described in this book will help your child to avoid this build up, such as:

- Taking regular time for relaxation;
- Maintaining hobbies and interests;
- Healthy eating;
- Healthy sleep habits;
- Keeping a sense of humour;
- Practising Gratitude;
- Putting events into perspective;
- Volunteering;
- Turning to support networks;
- Seeking the advice of adults or professionals when needed.

Whilst these will not prevent a stress build-up, they will help to stop a child feeling overwhelmed by their emotions. It gives them a bank of strategies to turn to, so that when they start to recognise the symptoms building up they can deploy them.

Key points from this chapter

- Stress is a common experience for adolescents.
- Siblings contribute to this stress.
- Social lives and romantic relationships also contribute.
- High levels of stress over time have a negative impact on the body.
- Young people need to be taught how to deal with stress and also techniques for avoiding the build-up to stress.

Coping with Stress

A.W.O.L. the missing teenage brain

Social Lives

Peer and friendship groups are an important part of a young person's life. Around the age of 10-12 years, children start to form small cliques and differentiate 'friends' from 'peers' in their year group. By the age of 12-13, the need to conform to what their friends like/dislike is at its peak. Friends are seen as just a good form of support as their parents, with the reliance on parents reducing over the next few years. By 15 young people, see their same-sex friends as their main form of support.

However, at the same time, social lives also cause no end of problems for adolescents. Many social problems are dealt with by the frontal lobes, which are effectively shut down during puberty. This means that many minor social difficulties that can rationally and easily be dealt with become major dramas and provoke an emotional response. Because of the problems with problem-solving due to the brain changes, it can also cause difficulties with solving normal friendship dilemmas.

The frontal lobes contain an area important in both the production of speech and the comprehension of speech. Think how many major social issues are caused by the misinterpretation of what someone said.

With continuous access to friends and peers through the internet and social media, social issues are more prevalent for young people and it is likely they will need more support throughout this period. Help your child by being the soundboard for them – keep the door open for them to be able to turn to you to help sort these problems before they react emotionally.

Key points from this chapter

- During early adolescence, young people start to differentiate friends from peers.
- The brain changes can cause social difficulties to become major problems or cause emotional responses.
- This is combined with difficulties with normal problem-solving.
- Comprehension and production of speech are also affected by the changes in the brain.
- That constant access to social media has an impact on any social issues.

A.W.O.L. the missing teenage brain

Romantic Relationships

During early adolescence, romantic relationships often begin as an extra special friendship. During this initial phase, relationships are experimental and short-term. By middle adolescence, these have developed into a status symbol and are closely connected to the views of their friendship group. It is not until early adulthood that romantic relationships become socially intimate. Partners start to become a reliable form of emotional support, with a joint focus on the relationship – separating it from the peer status held before. As they mature, this develops into a need to bond, which settles into longer-term relationships.

This journey can be incredibly stressful, with turbulent twists and turns along the way. We all remember an early rejection, a devastating break up or social issues surrounding our pick of a partner.

The way people handle early romantic relationships is based on their relationships with those around them and the relationships they have seen between others. This includes both parent-child relationships and peer relationships.

Furman & Wehner (1994, 1997) identified four patterns of behaviour in romantic relationships, these are:

> Attachment – the need for a secure relationship with another;
> Caregiving – the need to be cared for and care for another;
> Affiliation – companionship and sharing of pleasurable time together;
> Sexual systems – the need to meet sexual desires and reproduce.

Other factors that influences young people are those of gender and sexual identity. These add another layer of complexity to the early steps into relationships.

As with so many of the factors affecting your child, it is important that you maintain a relationship where they can have open and frank discussions with you, without the fear of being judged. They may be concerned about how you will react or your own beliefs, but for your child it is important they can access that support. Often, your child may want to turn to someone else to have these discussions, it is equally as important that you recognise if this is the case and signpost them to people they can speak to, such as another relative, a counsellor or mentor.

Key points from this chapter

- The development of romantic relationships happens in stages.
- The first stage is an extra special friendship.
- The second stage is as status within their social group.
- The third, is the development of social intimacy.
- Initially romantic relationships are based on what people have seen or experienced.
- Behaviour in romantic relationships can be associated with the need for attachment, caregiving, affiliation and sexual systems.
- It is important for adults to be a form of support for young people.

Romantic Relationships

A.W.O.L. the missing teenage brain

Technology

The adolescent use of gadgets is a constant source of frustration for many adults. Children appear addicted to having a device in their hands and often do not seem to know how to switch off from them.

Many young people use technology for education, gaming, recreational, relaxational and social reasons. Often they will be doing multiple things at the same time. They may be doing a piece of homework, whilst listening to a podcast and chatting to their friends. Younger generations certainly believe they are better at multi-tasking.

The use of technology can be a useful support mechanism for the mental wellbeing of a young person, isolating them away from the Internet and their online support networks can actually be detrimental. However, too much access to technology is also bad for them, so finding the right line can be difficult.

First of all, it will aid sleep to not have phones or tablets (or similar devices) with them in bed overnight, their presence alone can interrupt the sleep cycle.

Secondly, it is important to have regular time away from screens, ideally several times a day. Certainly, the last hour or so before bedtime will again help with sleep.

Having regular breaks from screens will help to break the dopamine loop cycle we spoke about earlier in the book. The build-up of hormones can lead to a determination to keep going with a problem or complete a difficult level on a game. It can be far more beneficial, particularly if trying to solve a problem, to go and clear your head.

The time to do this is when they start to experience some of these symptoms:

- Tired eyes,
- Headache,
- An increased stress or agitation level,

- An increase in the amount of flicking between things to seek stimulation or reward,
- Less patience,
- More frustration.

Key points from this chapter

- Young people use various forms of technology at the same time.
- Technology can be a useful support mechanism for young people.
- Devices in the room at night can interrupt the sleep cycle.
- It is important young people have regular breaks from technology.
- Young people need to recognise when they need to take a break from devices.

Technology

A.W.O.L. the missing teenage brain

Online relationships

Many adults have concerns about children being groomed, trolled or bullied online. There are many scare stories to hear about or read. The internet can be an unfiltered domain and, as with life, there are always people to be avoided. Teaching your child to say no thank you or ignore undesirable people online is just as important as them learning about how to do it in the school playground. Ask your child about what they have seen or heard of, it is likely to be more than you expect and will give you a chance to open up the conversation, particularly if they have been cyberbullied and have not found a way of seeking help from you.

Online bullying is normally carried out by someone who knows the victim. Unfortunately, bullying is often linked to someone's own feelings of insecurity and so this is projected onto the victim. It can be hard for young people to see this at times and in order to protect themselves they may avoid the bullies or join them in bullying others so they do not stand out. The problem is with online bullying is that you cannot get away from it. If someone is directing comments at you, then you keep receiving notifications when they do. Issues that years ago would have been left in the playground are now 24 hour battles for young people, there is no divide with technology. Be there for your child and if they are concerned, teach them to turn off notifications, change their privacy settings or even walk away from the screen and go to do something to take their mind off it.

Never dismiss the impact of online trolling or bullying, it can be very targeted and incredibly painful. Very often young people who are victims may avoid telling adults because they may be ashamed or not sure what to do. It is vital that we adults check in regularly with young people and offer support when necessary. See the chapter on support networks later in this book for more guidance on this support.

Key points from this chapter

- It is important to teach young people to recognise they are being groomed or trolled and how to deal with it.
- Online bullying is often carried out by someone who knows the young person.
- Trolling and online bullying can be very painful for a young person.

A.W.O.L. the missing teenage brain

Part Four Strategies for Resilience and Good Mental Health

A.W.O.L. the missing teenage brain

Healthy Sleep

For your children to get a good night's sleep and keep to a sensible routine of going to bed and feeling refreshed in the morning a solution is to trick the brain into releasing the sleep drug earlier in the evening. This process is called *entrainment* and involves making the subconscious think it is later in the evening than it actually is and release melatonin earlier. The key things you can do to help are:

- Use bright lights in the morning to help rouse your sleeping child.
- Dim the lights in the evening once you have had dinner, so it starts to feel like it is later.
- Tell them to avoid caffeine in the afternoon to allow it to have left their system, rather than keep them awake.

- Have at least an hour without screens before bed to allow the dopamine level to drop and reduce the impact of the blue light delaying the sleep cycle.
- Suggest they have a hot milky drink just before bed (as it contains tryptophan, which causes sleepiness).
- Allow your child to sleep in at the weekend if they can and use an alarm clock during term time. By letting them sleep in at the weekend they will be able to catch up on those lost hours of sleep if they still end up going to bed late.

Discuss with young people how they cope with interrupted sleep cycles. If they adopt two different sleep cycles (weekdays and weekends), then it is important that they are able to use this as a coping mechanism.

Healthy Sleep

Key points from this chapter

- Use entrainment to train the brain to release melatonin earlier in the evening.
- This may involve:
    - Using bright lights in the morning,
    - Dimming lights in the evening,
    - Avoiding caffeine,
    - Having hot milky drink before bed,
    - Time away from screens.
- Discuss with them their different sleep cycles as a coping mechanism.

A.W.O.L. the missing teenage brain

Healthy Eating

Children may want to gorge themselves on junk food. It is recommended that as much as 45-65% of daily calories are carbohydrates during the teenage years. However, much junk food only provides simple carbs, which release energy over a short period of time, whereas the recommendation relates to complex carbs. Simple carbs have short chains of one or two sugar molecules, which are broken down easily by the body. Other examples of simple carbs (apart from sugar) are fruits, milk and milk products. Complex carbohydrates include more vitamins and fibre, and are released over a longer period of time; this is because the sugar chains are far longer. Examples include green vegetables, wholegrain rice and oats, potatoes, sweet potatoes, corn, pumpkin, beans or lentils.

Diet can also affect their sleep. Sugar can delay sleep and also causes the skin to become greasier (and increase the likelihood of acne). The body produces more blood sugar to combat the effects of sleep deprivation. If that sleep deprivation was caused by sugar in the first place, then this could become a vicious cycle.

Teenagers will also need about 2 litres of water a day (as do adults). This can increase if they are exercising, or the atmosphere is humid or warm. Dehydration, or not having enough water, can cause headaches, dizziness, dry skin and tiredness. The brain is approximately 85% water and studies have shown that as little as a 1% level of dehydration can affect cognitive performance by as much as 5% (e.g. Armstrong et al, 2012, Ganio et al, 2011).

We therefore need to ensure children recognise the importance of keeping themselves hydrated and how to recognise when they are starting to become dehydrated. Two litres of water equates to, it is at least 8 cups. If someone drinks sugary drinks, they should be aware that sugar dehydrates us.

Teenagers and preteens will benefit from calcium (in milk, yoghurt, cheese, soy, tofu, spring greens, kale, figs, almonds or beans) to assist the construction of healthy bones during their growth spurt. Finally vitamin D aides bone and muscles development, apart from being obtained from sunlight, it is found in oily fish, red meat, liver, egg yolks, fat spreads and some breakfast cereals. As periods begin, girls will also need iron in their diet, this can be obtained from baked beans, beans, lentils, eggs or enriched cereals. Vitamin C aids the absorption of iron.

Key points from this chapter

- Teenagers may require high amounts of carbohydrates.
- These should include complex carbs.
- Simple carbs break down to sugar, which can affect sleep.
- Teens need high amounts of water.
- They also require calcium, vitamin D and if they are female additional iron.

Healthy Eating

A.W.O.L. the missing teenage brain

Healthy Exercise

It is recommended that young people do at least 60 minutes of exercise a day and three times a week. This should include muscular workouts. The daily exercises might include activities like walking, running, cycling or sports. The tri-weekly exercise should consist of activities to build muscle and bone density, such as going to the gym, skipping, swimming, aerobics or even for younger children playing on playground equipment.

A higher frequency of exercise in adolescents is linked to better psychological wellbeing and releases feel good endorphins. There is also evidence that regular exercise helps combat major depression, although this is limited if the young person is not self-motivated to keep the exercise going. Long-term studies have shown that exercise was linked with increased self-worth, perceived efficiency of heart and lungs, plus their own view of their body image.

The important thing for young people is the maintenance of their attitude towards exercise and physical activity. Here are a few strategies to help them:

- Set reasonable goals, don't try and over exert themselves at the start;
- Do different types of exercise, this helps to keep the interest level up;
- Chose enjoyable exercises, if you find running boring, but like cycling, then do more of that;
- Make it sociable, invite a friend or do something together;
- Monitor the impact of exercise on their mood; remember which types of exercise are good for picking them up when they feel down.

Key points from this chapter

- Young people should do 60 minutes of exercise a day.
- This should be supplemented by high-intensity workouts three times a week.
- Higher frequencies of exercise are linked to improved mental wellbeing.
- Adults can support young people in developing the right attitude to physical exercise.

A.W.O.L. the missing teenage brain

Goal Setting

An important part of getting the most out of the teenage years is recognising things they want to achieve and how to set goals to get there. There are several things you could do to help your child set their goals. The first is to get them to make a timeline of their lives over the next few months/years. What is it they plan to do or want to achieve in that time? How will they know they are moving towards it? Write or draw on key milestones along the way.

Another method commonly used is to make a vision board – a pin board (or online equivalent) of things they want to do or achieve. Print off pictures from the internet or cut them out of magazines. Put a date by each one to make sure that your child can be focussed on achieving the goal by that date. They can

A.W.O.L. the missing teenage brain

then even replace the images with photos of them achieving each of them.

For someone who is stuck on how to achieve his or her goal, you can use another technique. Get them to think about the massive end goal. Visualise themselves achieving it, what is happening? How does it feel? What do they see? What do they hear?

Now they are using their senses to imagine it, ask them what they did just before they got there. That is a smaller goal on the path; get them to write it down. Now ask them what they did just before that, and so on. Eventually track it back to the present time; you will end up with a series of goals culminating in the main one they want to achieve:

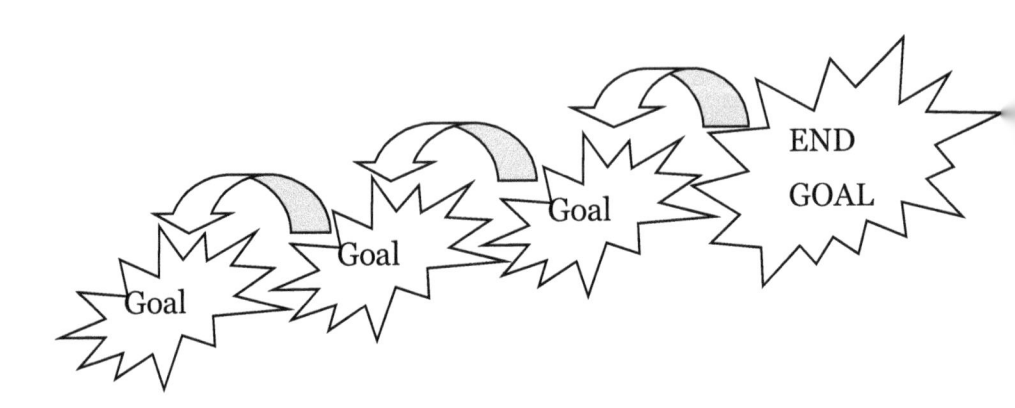

Key points from this chapter

- It is important that young people can recognise what they want to achieve.
- Adults can help young people to identify what they want to achieve.
- Vision boards can be used to set goals.
- Visualisation can be used to imagine how to overcome blocks.
- This can be used to break down the large goal into smaller goals.

A.W.O.L. the missing teenage brain

Self-Motivation

Self-motivation may need to be channelled in young people. Due to the changes in the brain, adolescents are prone to risk-taking behaviour and they may be attracted to the reward or novelty of risks.

Ernst, Pine and Hardin (2006) developed a model to explain this phenomenon. The first is an area of the *hypothalamus* known as the *nucleus accumbens*. This is the pleasure centre and the desire to stimulate it is particularly strong in teenagers. The second factor is that the brain has a weak harm-avoidance system (controlled by the *amygdala*) during this period. These are both then combined with a weak and inefficient supervisory control system in the *prefrontal cortex*. We explained the rationale behind the reasons for this earlier in the book, but when it comes to the current topic, it is clear that for some children they may need some steering.

Some children need help to learn to do homework for themselves, or for their exams. Others need help with finding new friends, maintaining their social life or persevering with a hobby or club. That support is likely to be time-consuming and intensive in the early days, adults often need to model or show children how to be self-motivated. This is also a good opportunity to teach them about financial planning and how they can earn money and save up towards goals if they are self-motivated (and will stimulate their pleasure/reward centre described above).

When it comes to personal goals, if a young person procrastinates, nothing will get done. Adults need to get children to think about what they want to do, to achieve and help them plan how they can get there. Our role is to encourage them to work hard so they can reach whatever goal they have.

There is a discipline that goes into achieving goals. Just the same as for gold winning athletes, it has been the years of giving up social time, getting up early and training that helped them to achieve the medal, not just turning up for the race on the day.

Focus and determination are important, as we described earlier with exercise, as the brain will often find reasons why something does not have to be done. There is no point in starting something to give up after a few weeks, but again children need to learn this. This sense of perseverance and keeping going through thick and thin is a life skill that will help them with their adult lives.

It is easy to see failure as black and white, however failure is actually positive. Failure gives people a mistake to learn a lesson from and many children learn by persisting until they get it right. Help your children see that they either need more practise at it, try again because their first attempt was not their best or realise this is not where their strengths lie. Self-motivation is saying to yourself 'I am going to do this thing. I am going to get stuck in and keep going.'

Key points from this chapter

- Self-motivation may need to be supported during adolescence.
- Young people will be attracted towards risk-taking behaviour.
- They may need support with understanding how to manage academic expectations.
- Adults can support young people to identify their own personal goals and how to achieve them.
- Achieving a goal often needs discipline.
- Young people need to see failure as an opportunity for learning.

Self-Motivation

A.W.O.L. the missing teenage brain

Relaxation

Relaxation is a vital part of maintaining positive mental health. Allowing the brain to enjoy being in the moment and feel happy with the current activity, whilst letting the stresses and strains flow out of them.

The key difference between a relaxing activity and a hobby is to do with engagement. Hobbies are often activities that involve being absorbed in an engaging activity or something that the young person is passionate about. They often raise the young person's pulse whilst doing them and hopefully involve the release of the feel good drug *endorphins*.

Relaxing activities on the other hand are more related to reducing stress levels, and are more related to restoring the emotional and hormonal balance in the body. They are often pastimes that allow the mind to enjoy the moment and forget the current stresses or strains.

Relaxation activities are often an activity that does not involve much conscious thought:

- Spa days
- Reading
- Jigsaws
- Colouring
- Painting
- Walks in the countryside
- Sorting paperwork
- Meditation
- Yoga
- Gratitude

There are many other activities that can be relaxing if done in a calm way, but at other times increase stress or become a hobby rather than a relaxation exercise.

These may include things like:

- Interests with family or friends
- Knitting
- Cross-stitch
- Running
- Card games like solitaire
- Sudoku
- Word searches

Mindfulness is a practice with origins in Buddhism. It is based on the concept of focussing the mind on the current moment or experience. Over the last fifty years, a number of psychological and clinical applications have been developed and there is an increasing research base showing the benefits. The American Psychological Association (apa.org) identify these as:

- Reduced focus on negative life events;
- Reduced stress;
- Boosting working memory;
- Increased focus;
- Ability to distance oneself from emotionally upsetting events;
- Brain flexibility;
- Better satisfaction in relationships; or
- Increased immune functioning.

Examples of mindful activities may be something as simple as studying an object in great detail, breathing exercises, studying your smile in the mirror, visualisation exercises, defining daily goals. Others are more complex and require training, such as something called a body scan, where the individual relaxes and works focuses on their whole body small sections at a time.

Our children need to recognise what helps them to relax; how they can make sure they do it regularly and how to be in the moment. For you spend time sharing how you relax and let your wandering thoughts go whilst you enjoy being in the moment.

Relaxation

Key points from this chapter

- Relaxation is important for positive mental wellbeing.
- Hobbies are different from relaxation activities.
- Relaxation activities may include:
    - Spa days
    - Reading
    - Jigsaws
    - Colouring
    - Painting
    - Walks in the countryside
    - Sorting paperwork
    - Meditation
    - Yoga
    - Gratitude
- Mindfulness has positive effects on mental wellbeing.

A.W.O.L. the missing teenage brain

Support Networks

There are two ways that support networks aid positive mental health in someone identified by Cohen and Wills. The first is about providing positive well-being all of the time and the second is known as 'stress-buffering', applying when the individual is undergoing stress or poor mental health. Within the former, there are several ways of affecting someone's life according to Cohen, Underwood and Gottleib: social influence, positive affective states and neuroendocrine responses.

Social influence relates to the behaviours of other people influencing the health-promoting activity of the person themselves, for example exercise. Being part of a strong social network will also affect someone's sense of purpose, belonging, security and self-worth.

Thoits (1986) suggested support networks affects the way people respond to stress. She felt that if someone feels they have people to turn to, then it will reduce the negative responses they experience. The availability or access to support as the person moves forward can either reduce the negative emotional reaction, or reduce the behavioural and physiological responses they experience.

Whomever your child decides they want the support of they need to know that if they say anything that requires a social worker or police intervention then the adult they have confided in has to report it. For example if your child talks about being groomed, abused, radicalised or a victim of a crime. They do not need to be scared as these professionals are better equipped to help them with these situations.

Over the next few pages, we will go over the different support networks surrounding young people.

Types of conversation

There are two types of conversation that adults will use as they move from a disciplinarian role to more of a life coach or mentor. The first is that of an information-giving nature, the second an active-listening conversation.

With both conversations, you will want to begin by making your young person feel safe, go somewhere where you will not be interrupted or their sibling will not listen or join in, reassure them that you want to give them advice, not tell them what to do. It may be your child will come to you, or otherwise you may pick up something's wrong and ask if they would like a chat.

With informative conversations, your role is to listen (mostly in silence) to your child's concerns or worries. You then want to give them the facts without your opinion to begin with. This again helps your child to feel a sense of trust in your advice. It is only then, that you share your opinions or views and explain your rationale. The ultimate decision is with your child and you are their guide through the complexities.

Active-listening conversations are more focussed on helping your child to solve a problem in their lives. Here, you will ask an open question and use silence as you listen to your child, for example "How are you getting on with Azmat now?"

Often people make a simple mistake at this point, they do not give their child time to think and process their thoughts. Instead, they try to be helpful and suggest things their child could be thinking and so for the child it becomes about agreeing or disagreeing with the adult.

So, to put it simply, once you have made your child feel safe, ask an open question about the problem and then sit in silence whilst they think and begin to speak through the issue. Remember, if they need help clarifying their thoughts, they will ask for it (for example "I don't know what you mean?"). Very often, this process will help them to be able to speak through the options and come up with their next course of action. At other times, you will need to suggest things they might do once you have listened to them explain the situation.

Parents

Parents hold a unique part in the support networks for young people. Early in adolescence, they identify their parents as their main form of support and during middle adolescence as an equal form of support as their friends.

Apart from providing advice, the other thing that young people will rely on their parents for is the modern world (which is very different from when you were young). Leaving aside technology, attitude is very different too. An example of this is your child's friendship network is likely to include international friends made over the internet.

Gone are the days of physically seeing friends or sharing one phone in the hallway, today's young people communicate far more effectively using social media. This has an impact on their growing brain and the chemicals going through their body. They have grown up in a world where you message someone, you can see the moment they read it and whether they are typing a reply. The immediacy of this causes no end of social problems as emotional, ill thought out messages are exchanged, sometimes leading to arguments or bullying.

Accessibility of devices means that things that would have been left at school are now brought into your child's bedroom. The downtime that people all need after an incident actually turns into a continuation or acceleration of the initial problem.

Young people also are growing up in a world where there is no problem with questioning established ways of doing things or thinking differently about things. Their point of view may surprise or even alarm your beliefs at times, whilst they do not see anything wrong in what they have just said. The world is a lot more accepting of different viewpoints and as a parent, you are placed in the position where you have been telling a child what to do, but as they approach adolescence, you have to understand their point of view and help them to make the right decision.

This also means that all of the issues you encountered when you were going through puberty are even more complex in today's world. This means that often parents will feel out of their depth at times and need to ask their child to explain to them. Given the shift in the world over the last fifteen years, there is nothing wrong with this and in fact, it can help to strengthen the trust in your relationship with your child as you both learn from each other.

Teachers

Whilst teacher training does not cover mental health, there is an increasing recognition of the role teachers play in supporting mental health. Over the past few years there have been a number of training courses and conferences held for teachers, although many teachers lack confidence in dealing with mental health difficulties,.

As with parents, there are two types of conversation that teachers may have with young people. The first is information-giving and the other is an active-listening conversation. These are covered in the last few pages in more detail.

In 2016, Capp and others summarised the research relating to different adults' relationships with adolescents and the impact on mental health. They highlight the importance of supportive school climates in protecting children against psychological risks, whereas for pupils with poor relationships with their teachers there is a higher risk of problems associated with drugs, mental health problems and academic difficulties.

It is important that parents foster positive relationships with teachers and school staff. We are in a time when the relationship has shifted from either the parents or teachers being responsible for a child's wellbeing, to recognition that this is a partnership.

Parents can contribute to the relationship with teachers by modelling the relationship expectations for their children. Parents talking about teachers who mentored them or took them under their wing, will help a child understand that they were young once and also prompt the child to reflect on their relationships with their teachers. Whatever happens, adults talking about school and teachers in a positive way will give a subliminal message to a child about your relationship with them. We can all think about times the work done on building a relationship with a teacher is affected by a throw away comment about how bad the school/teacher/homework is.

Family

Extended family have often grown up in the same house as one of the child's parents and will understand the parent's viewpoints. This is particularly helpful if your child wants to seek advice about their home life. Aunts and Uncles are good people for a child to discuss the whole picture, being able to talk about home, friendships and school from an independent point of view. This almost gives them the ability to have an agenda-free conversation with your child. If your child enjoys spending time with another relative on a hobby, support and encourage him or her to maintain that relationship, especially during the stressful times they will experience.

Children often feel close to their grandparents; it may be that your child feels that they would be a good person to speak to about a particular problem. At other times, it may be that they are taken under the wing of one of their grandparents. Not only will these conversations give them a different viewpoint, but it will also help them to understand their heritage. This can be particularly important when it comes to thinking about why you as a parent insist on something or have a particular value. Very often understanding the reasons behind something can change the way people feel or react to a particular problem.

Support from families is important, particularly if your child is going through any issues or exploration around their own identity, gender or sexuality. A 2016 study by McConnell, Birkett and Mustanski looked at the mental health of lesbian, gay, bisexual and transgender adolescents. They found that young people who had high levels of family support reported less distress during adolescence and early adulthood.

Mentors

A mentor is someone who has experience in a particular area or has travelled a similar journey or path. They use this experience to help a mentee to overcome their barriers or blocks. There are many schools, colleges and organisations who provide mentors for young people. Mentoring sessions are confidential (unless there is a danger to someone or a child protection issue).

Research on a long-term study (DuBois & Silverthorn, 2005) has shown that mentoring performed better in education and work, reduced behaviour problems, increased mental well-being, better birth control use and higher levels of physical activity.

If your child has access to a mentor, they should have discussed with their mentor the kinds of things the mentor can assist them. If your child can share these with you, it will help you to know when it is appropriate to suggest which problems or difficulties to take to the mentor.

A.W.O.L. the missing teenage brain

Friends and romantic partners

As we discussed earlier in this book, adolescence is a period when a child moves from seeing their parents as the main form of support, to seeing their close friends as that support. By the end of adolescence, young people have shifted their position and see their romantic partners as the main person to turn to.

When you observe this, discuss with your child which friends they can trust with different problems. One may be good at relationship advice, another may be better with academic solutions. They will also need to consider whom they can trust with opening up to. As with adult social circles, this will vary depending on the topic of the advice sought.

A.W.O.L. the missing teenage brain

Other professionals

There will be times when your child does not want to come to you or needs advice about how to raise something with you (or how to manage you). During these times, they are likely to self-select a trusted person to speak to, including other adults and professionals.

Hamilton and Hamilton in the Handbook of Adolescent Psychology summarise important research in this area. One study from 1996 found that 82% of 3rd year college (equivalent to university 20-21 year olds) named at least one adult outside of the family when asked who their ten most important adults before starting at college. Another study they quote found that 56% of 12-14 year olds had asked an unrelated adult for help.

You may find your child consults other adults for support. Do not be surprised by this and as with other areas; help them to identify who it is good to turn to.

Key points from this chapter

- Support networks are important for avoiding mental health problems.
- Young people may consult different people for various problems they encounter.
- There are two different types of supportive conversation that adults might have with young people:
    - Information giving,
    - Active listening.
- Support may come from parents, teachers, wider family, mentors, friends and romantic partners, plus other professionals.
- Young people will view friends and romantic partners as important forms of support in later adolescence.

Support Networks

A.W.O.L. the missing teenage brain

Back Matter

A.W.O.L. the missing teenage brain

References and Further Reading

Books

Bailey, S. and Shooter, M. (Eds), (2009). *The Young Mind*, London: Transworld.

Curtis, R.D., (2018). *The Parent's Guide to the Modern World*, Southampton: The Kid Calmer.

Curtis, R.D., (2018). *The Young Person's Guide to the Modern World*, Southampton: The Kid Calmer.

Dweck, C., (2006). *Mindset: The New Psychology of Success*, New York: Ballatine Books.

Fowler, J.W. (1981). *Stages of Faith*, San Francisco: Harper & Row

Morgan, N., (2005). *Blame My Brain: the amazing teenage brain revealed*, London: Walker Books.

Research and Articles Referred to

American Psychiatric Association (2013). *Diagnostic and statistical manual of mental disorders: 5th Edition.* Arlington: American Psychiatric Association.

Armstrong, L.E., Ganio, M.S., Cada, D.J., Lee, E.C., McDermott, B.P., Klau, J.F., Jimenez, L., LeBellego, L., Chevillote, E. & Lieberman, H.R. (2012). Mild Dehydration Affects Mood in Healthy Young Women. *The Journal of Nutrition,* 142 (2), 382-388.

Blakemore, S.-J. and Choudhury, S. (2006). Development of the adolescent brain: implications for executive function and social cognition. *Journal of Child Psychology and Psychiatry,* 47: 296–312.

Blos, P. (1967). The Second Individuation Process of Adolescence. *The Psychoanalytic Study of the Child,* 22 (1), 162-186.

Brown, S.A., Tapert, S.F., Granholm, E. & Delis, D.C. (2000). Neurocognitive Functioning of Adolescents: Effects of Protracted Alcohol Use. *Alcoholism, Clinical and Experimental Research,* 24(2), 164-171.

Capp, G., Berkowitz, R., Sullivan, K., Astor, R.A., De Pedro, K., Gilreath, T.D., Benbenishty, R., & Rice, E. (2016). Adult Relationships in Multiple Contexts and Associations with

Adolescent Mental Health. *Research On Social Work Practice, 26*(6), 622-629.

Carskadon, M.A. (2011). Sleep in Adolescents: The Perfect Storm. *Pediatric Clinics of North America,* 58(3), 637-647.

Chandra, A. & Batada, A. (2006). Exploring Stress and Coping Among Urban African American Adolescents: The Shifting the Lens Study. *Preventing Chronic Disease*, April.

Christ, G.H., (2000). Impact of Development on Children's Mourning. *Cancer Practice,* 8 (2). 72-81.

Cohen S., Underwood L.G. & Gottlieb B.H. (2000). *Social Support Measurement and Intervention. A Guide for Health and Social Scientists.* New York: Oxford University Press.

Cohen S. & Wills T.A. (1985). Stress, social support, and the buffering hypothesis. *Psychological Bulletin,* 98(2), 310–357.

Connery, H.S., Corliss, J. & Allison, K.C. (Eds) (2011). *Alcohol use and abuse.* Harvard Health Publications.

Cotman, C.W., Berchtold, N.C. & Christie, L. (2007). Exercise builds brain health: key roles of growth factor cascades and inflammation. *Trends in Neurosciences,* 30 (9), 464-472.

Crowley, S.J. & Carskadon, M.A. (2007). Sleep, circadian rhythms and delayed phase in adolescence. *Sleep Medicine,* 8 (6), 602-612.

Dahl R.E. (2003). Beyond raging hormones: the tinderbox in the teenage brain. *Cerebrum,* 5 (3), 7–22.

De Bellis, M.D., Clark, D. B., Beers, S. R., Soloff, P. H., Boring, A. M., Hall, J. Kersh, A. & Keshavan, M. S. (2000). Hippocampal Volume in Adolescent-Onset Alcohol Use Disorders. *The American Journal of Psychiatry*, 157 (5), 737-744.

Department of Health (2009). *Guidance on the consumption of alcohol by children and young people*, DoH. Available at http://www.cph.org.uk/wp-content/uploads/2013/09/Guidance-on-the-consumption-of-alcohol-by-children-and-young-people.pdf.

DuBois, D.L. & Silverthorn, N. (2005). Natural Mentoring Relationships and Adolescent Health: Evidence From a National Study. *American Journal of Public Health*, 95 (3), 518-524.

Dumontheil, I., Apperly, I.A., Blakemore, S.J. (2009). Online usage of theory of mind continues to develop in late adolescence. *Developmental Science*, 13 (2), 331-338.

Ellis, B.J., McFadyen-Ketchum, S., Dodge, K.A., Pettit, G.A., & Bates, J.E. (1999). Quality of early family relationships and individual differences in the timing of pubertal maturation in girls: A longitudinal test of an evolutionary model. *Journal of Personality and Social Psychology*, 77, 387– 401.

Ernst, M., Pine, D.S., & Hardin, M. (2006) Triadic model of the neurobiology of motivated behavior in adolescence. *Psychological Medicine,* 36(3), 299-312.

Ganio, M.S., Armstrong, L.E., Casa, D.J., McDermott, B.P., Lee, E.C., Yamamoto, L.M., Marzano, S., Lopez, R.M., Jimenez, L., LeBellego, L., Chevillotte, E. & Lieberman, H.R. (2011). Mild dehydration impairs cognitive performance and mood of men. *British Journal of Nutrition,* 106 (10), 1535-1543.

Ge, X., Conger, R.D., & Elder, G.H. (2001a). Pubertal transition, stressful life events, and the emergence of gender differences in depressive symptoms during adolescence. *Developmental Psychology,* 37, 404– 417.

Ge, X., Conger, R.D., & Elder, G.H. (2001b). The relation between puberty and psychological distress in adolescent boys. *Journal of Research on Adolescence,* 11, 49– 70.

Giedd, J.N., Blumenthal, J., Jeffries, N.O., Castellanos, F.X., Liu, H., Zijdenbos, A., Paus, T., Evans, A.C., & Rapoport, J.L. (1999). Brain development during childhood and adolescence: A longitudinal MRI study. *Nature Neuroscience,* 2, 861–863.

Hamilton S.F. & Hamilton M.A. (2004). Contexts for mentoring: Adolescent-adult relationships in workplaces and communities. *Handbook of Adolescent Psychology,* 2, 395–428.

Helzer J.E., Burnam A. & McEvoy L.T. (1991). Alcohol abuse and dependence: a report from the Epidemiologic Catchment Area study. In: Robins L.N. & Regier D.A. (Eds) (1991). *Psychiatric disorders in America* (pp 81-115). New York: Free Press.

Kaltiala-Heino R., Kosunen E. & Rimpelä M. (2003). Pubertal timing, sexual behaviour and self-reported depression in middle adolescence. *Journal of Adolescence*, 26 (5), 531-545.

Kelleher, I., Connor, D., Clarke, M.C., Devlin, N., Harley, M. & Cannon, M. (2012) Prevalence of psychotic symptoms in childhood and adolescence: a systematic review and meta-analysis of population-based studies. *Psychological Medicine*, 42 (9), 1857-1863.

Kim, K., Smith, P.K., and Palermiti, A.L. (1997). Conflict in childhood and reproductive development. *Evolution and Human Behavior*, 18, 109-142.

Kosunen, E., Kaltiala-Heino, R., Rimpelä, M. & Laippala, P. (2003). Risk-taking sexual behaviour and self-reported depression in middle adolescence – a school-based survey. *Child: Care, Health and Development*, 29 (5), 337-344.

LeCloux, M., Maramaldi, P., Thomas, K., & Wharff, E. (2016). Family Support and Mental Health Service Use Among Suicidal Adolescents. *Journal Of Child & Family Studies*, 25(8), 2597-260.

McConnell, E.A., Birkett, M., & Mustanski, B. (2016). Families Matter: Social Support and Mental Health Trajectories Among Lesbian, Gay, Bisexual, and Transgender Youth. *Journal Of Adolescent Health*, 59(6), 674-680.

Marcia, J.E. (1966). Development and Validation of Ego-Identity Status. *Journal of Personality and Social Psychology*, 3(5), 551-558.

National Institute on Alcohol Abuse and Alcoholism (2017). *Underage Drinking* [pamphlet]. Retrieved from https://pubs.niaaa.nih.gov/publications/underagedrinking/Underage_Fact.pdf.

NHS (2006) *Statistics on Young People and Drug Misuse: England, 2006*. Retrieved from https://digital.nhs.uk/data-and-information/publications/statistical/statistics-on-drug-misuse/2006-young-people.

Purvis, D., Robinson, Merry, S, & Watson, P. (2006). Acne, depression and suicide in teenagers: A cross-sectional survey of New Zealand secondary school students. *Journal of Paediatrics and Child Health*, 42 (12), 793-796.

Saarikallio, S. & Erkkilä, J. (2007). The role of music in adolescents' mood regulation. *Psychology of Music*, 35 (1), 88-109.

Susman, E.J. & Dorn, L.D. (2012). Puberty Its Role in Development. In Weiner, I.B., Lerner, R.M., Easterbrooks,

M.A. & Mistry, J. *Handbook of Psychology: Developmental Psychology* (pp. 289-320). Hoboken: Wiley & Sons.

Swartzwelder, H.S., Wilson, W.A. & Tayyeb, M.I. (1995). Differential Sensitivity of NMDA Receptor-Mediated Synaptic Potentials to Ethanol in Immature Versus Mature Hippocampus. *Alcoholism: Clinical and Experimental Research*, 19(2), 320-323.

Thoits, P.A. (1986). Social support as coping assistance. *Journal of Consulting and Clinical Psychology*, 54, 416–423.

van Jaarsveld C.H., Fidler J.A., Simon AE.. & Wardle J. (2007). Persistent impact of pubertal timing on trends in smoking, food choice, activity, and stress in adolescence. *Psychosomatic Medicine*, 69 (8), 798-806.

Willis, C.A. (2002). The Grieving Process in Children: Strategies for Understanding, Educating, and Reconciling Children's Perceptions of Death. *Early Childhood Education Journal*, 29 (4). 221-226.

Yurgelun-Todd, D. (2007). Emotional and cognitive changes during adolescence. *Current Opinion in Neurobiology*, 17 (2), 251-257.

References and Further Reading

A.W.O.L. the missing teenage brain

About the Author

Richard Daniel Curtis is an internationally renowned TV behaviour expert, passionate about helping millions around the world.

He has founded The Mentoring School, an award-winning training service to develop mentoring skills. Richard is also the founder of multi-award winning special needs support service The Root Of It.

The former teacher is known for his impact with turning around some of the most extreme behaviours and is consulted about the behaviour and performance of both adults and children. His work with children alone is said to have personally influenced the lives of over half a million.

Author of The Curtis Scale, a tool to assess the social and emotional development of children, Richard's work has had an impact in 5 continents. He has written 10 books, including *Gratitude at Home, Gratitude in Primary Schools, Gratitude in Secondary Schools and Higher Education, The Parent's Guide to the Modern World, The Young Person's Guide to the Modern World, 101 Tips for Parents, 101 More Tips for Parents* and *101 Behaviour Tips for Parents*; he has also co-authored *Boosting Positive Mental Health in Teens* with children's life coach

About the Author

Naomi Richards and *The Gifted Introvert* with Mary Jane Boholst.

Richard lives in Southampton with his girlfriend and their baby son.

Website - www.thekidcalmer.com
Twitter - @thekidcalmer
Facebook – facebook.com/thekidcalmer
LinkedIn - linkedin.com/in/richard-daniel-curtis

A.W.O.L. the missing teenage brain